Copyright © Victor S Weeks (
All rights reserved. No part of
reproduced, stored on a retrieval system, or transmitted in any form or by any means, without prior permission of the publishers.

ISBN: 0-9554724-0-7
ISBN: 978-0-9554724-0-4

Cover Picture: The Cotton Tree has been on this site since the time of the arrival of the Nova Scotian Settlers in 1792, from Canada.

Cover Design: Matthew Gill

Printed and bound by:
Mail & Print Direct Ltd, 17 Manvers Business Park,
High Hazels Road, Cotgrave,
Nottingham NG12 3GZ

Publisher:
Palm Tree Publishers UK
2 Bingham Road, Cotgrave, Nottingham NG12 3JR
Tel: 07710 376754

E-mail: victorokrafosmart@btinternet.com

Okrafo-Smart Family: Over a Century in the Lives of a Liberated African Family, 1816-1930

by

VICTOR S WEEKS OKRAFO-SMART M.A.

Dedication

To the memory of Rev. John Weeks who played such an important role in the lives of my ancestors at Regent Village, Sierra Leone between 1824 and 1855.

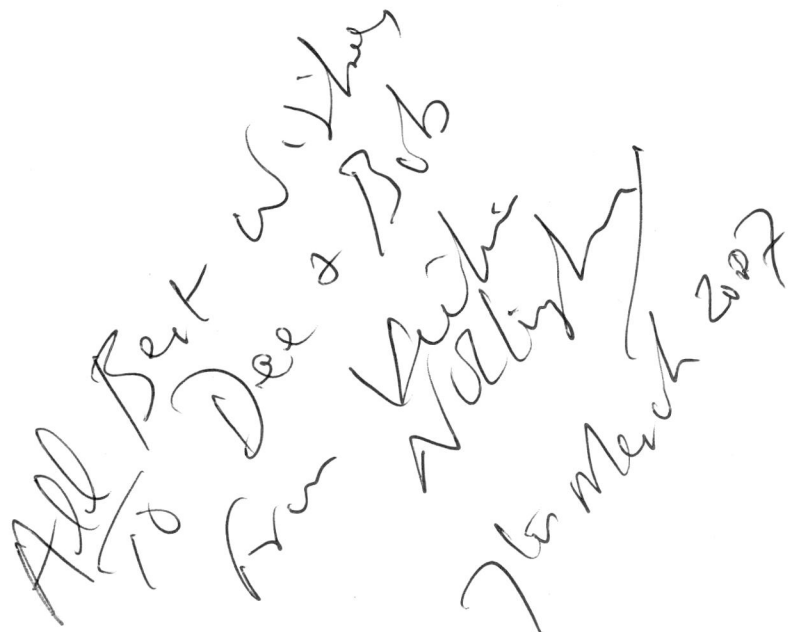

Introduction

When Victor Okrafo-Smart, a member of a distinguished Sierra Leone Krio family, left Queens Medical Centre, Nottingham, on early retirement, he decided to devote his partial retirement to researching his family history and contacted me to ask for advice. I was delighted to hear about his project and was able to give him references to documents in various archive collections which would be of use to him. He went about his work systematically, first taking a Master's degree to learn the skills of historical study and then starting research on his own, helped by his wife Ruth.

Together they discovered documents of extraordinary interest, notably in the archives of the Church Missionary Society, with which his family had a close connection, and in the voluminous files of the Freetown newspapers. The CMS archives included the detailed journals kept by one of his great-uncles who was a missionary in what is now Nigeria from 1868-76. The newspapers provided impressive articles by his grandfather on political and agricultural subjects. To these he added family traditions and reminiscences. His enjoyable narrative, enriched by many well-chosen illustrations, holds the story together readably, bringing to life the ideas and activities of his family members and, in addition, making a valuable contribution to the historiography of Sierra Leone.

Christopher Fyfe
Reader in African History (retired)
University of Edinburgh

Preface

The history of the Okrafo-Smart family Freetown, Sierra Leone.

My family history is a theme dear to my heart. This is a fascinating story of my ancestors, the first of whom arrived in Freetown, Sierra Leone about 1816 from Nigeria. The circumstances of his arrival in Sierra Leone are fully illustrated in the first chapter.

It is not known whether he came to Freetown from Nigeria on his own or whether he was in the company of his family members. In the introduction of his book *"An Innocent in Britain"* by Dr. Robert Wellesley-Cole, a descendant, he wrote "Descendant of an African prince who was kidnapped, rescued and settled in Sierra Leone"[1].

He was popular and well respected in the village of Regent where he settled. He died in 1837 in the presence of missionary Rev. John Weeks. In Weeks' journal he mentioned that up to four hundred people attended the funeral[2]. The number of mourners reflected the high esteem and respect of Okoroafor.

Pursuing the research of my family history, I have made extensive use of material sources at Colindale Library, the Public Records Officer, London, missionary documents at The Heslop Library, Birmingham University. My special thanks go to Mr. Christopher Fyfe, the former archivist of Sierra Leone, who provided me with various references and relevant materials, relating to three generations of the Smart family. They played important roles in Sierra Leone and West Africa, South Africa in education and missionary work. I have devoted a large section of the book on my late grandfather Francis Okrafor-Smart 1874 – 1930. He could arguably be described as a philanthropist, nationalist, entrepreneur and builder.

Extensive use has been made of journals of Rev. John Weeks who later became Bishop of Sierra Leone 1855 – 1857. A chapter is written on John Weeks who was to have a great influence and was much loved by the early generations of the Okrafor family.

Contents

	Page No
Chapter 1 Birth of a family – The arrival of Okoroafor-Smart First	1
Chapter 2 John Weeks	11
Chapter 3 An account of the early years of Regent by Christopher Fyfe	21
Chapter 4 John Smart Second – Headman Regent Village Catechist Niger Mission 1858-1859	31
Chapter 5 Frederick Weeks Smart 1841-1888 Niger Mission 1868-1876 Rev. Frederick Smart's Journals	37
Chapter 6 Rev. Frederick Smart's Letters Smart High School Left for The Gold Coast (Ghana)	77
Chapter 7 Francis John Smart 1841-1894 (Frederick twin brother) School Master, Government School Isle-de-Los	95

Chapter 8   101
    Francis (Great grandfather's children – Smart histories)

Chapter 9   111
    Francis's grandchildren –
    Children of his eldest daughter Elizabeth

Chapter 10   127
    Francis – my grandfather
- (i) City Hotel
- (ii) Health culture – buildings
- (iii) Director of Freetown Manufacturing Company
- (iv) Interview with His Excellency the Governor
- (v) Setting up various companies
- (vi) Setting up Sierra Leone Transportation Company of Freetown
- (vii) Ongoing integration by intermarriage between the Colony and Protectorate people
- (viii) England's Cattlefarm
- (ix) Social/cultural changes in Freetown
- (x) A Criminal Code
- (xi) National Congress of British West Africa (membership)
- (xii) Education versus Agriculture – his ideas
- (xiii) Farm acquisition – Smart Farm
- (xiv) Notes on Agriculture
- (xv) Regent Centenary Celebrations – his contribution
- (xvi) Prince of Wales' visit to Freetown 1925
- (xvii) Announcement of his death

Chapter 11   175
   Descendants of Francis Okrafor-Smart
      John Edowu
      Francis Balogun
      William Oreh and their children

Chapter 12   177
   Conclusion

Chapter 13   181
   Some observations of the Regent Census - 1831

   List of Illustrations   221
   Endnotes   223
   Index   227

1

The Birth of a Family

In 1807 the slave trade was abolished and Sierra Leone became a Crown colony in 1808. In order to regulate and enforce the actual abolition and prevention of the further supply of Africans to slavery, Britain set up institutions for the seizure and confiscation of slave ships in Freetown. As a result ethnic Africans captured and bound for slavery in the New World were released and resettled in Freetown and were known as "Liberated Africans".

Some came from the interior of Sierra Leone and others came from as far afield as Nigeria and Angola in the south. Between 1807 and 1870 about 84,000 Liberated Africans were resettled and rehabilitated in Sierra Leone.

Professor Akintola Wyse a well known Sierra Leonean historian has commented:

> 'Given the multi-ethnicity of the community and the varied culture and customs represented in the peninsula, it took some time before the Krio society assumed any form'[3]

The new arrivals were further relocated within various local villages in the peninsula. It is difficult to imagine thousands of new settlers with different languages, different cultures, in a strange land trying to adjust and rebuild their lives.

The policy of relocation of people who speak the same language was a good one and perhaps easier for administrative purposes. The idea also was to introduce these new settlers to and convert them to the Christian way of life. First of all a structured system of attachment and interrelationship had to be established. Hence the family unit promoted within the Christian faith.

Christian marriage was seen as substituting the African practice of polygamy. Only once polygamy was eradicated and marriage substituted could civilisation advance. Since marriage also implied the development of that basic want of civilisation – the family. The object was to encourage "the family" to develop in the British fashion.

The new arrivals were further relocated within various local villages in the peninsula. A despatch from Earl Bathurst, Colonial Secretary, on 23rd November 1826, in which he pointed out the objects to which he wished, the governor, Colonel Denham's attention to be directed and observed:

> 'That the only mode of attaching the Africans to their respective locations is by making them feel the advantages of property, and those which belong to domestic happiness; and for that purpose his Lordship suggests that marriage should be encouraged as much as possible amongst them'[4].

These resettled Africans were descendants of millions of Africans who had been taken away from Africa as a result of slavery as early as the late sixteenth century. Freetown was originally conceived as a place for providing a haven for freed slaves in the aftermath of the Somerset case in England which was taken to establish the principle that slavery could not legally exist within England and Wales. Noted philanthropists including, Granville Sharp, William Wilberforce, Clarkson and Macauley (all members of the Anglican Church) formerly set it up in 1787. Thus Sierra Leone was intended to provide a location back in Africa where rescued and freed slaves could be resettled and protected against further enslavement.

Sierra Leone thus had a particular symbolism for British philanthropists, especially those with an interest in Abolition. To these "enlightened" minds, the new settlement served as a solution to a British problem that had loaded the national, as well as the individuals' conscience with real guilt.

Thus it was within such circumstance that our ancestor Okoroafor arrived, probably about 1816. An Ibo from Nigeria. Oral history tells us that he came from a ruling class based in Imo state in what was Eastern Nigeria and was relocated at Regent. He would in the course of time, be influenced by two English officers for the rest of his life, John Weeks, later Bishop of Sierra Leone 1855 to 1857 and Samuel Smart Governor of Sierra Leone 1826 and 1828.

Regent would play a very important role in education and religion, important ingredients in the development and stability of early days in our history. To mention Regent without the Okrafor-Smart family was quite inappropriate. As would be seen later on, it was from Regent that members of my family set out on missionary and educational expeditions to

Isle-de-Los (Guinea) Ghana (then The Gold Coast), South Africa, and Nigeria.

The other official of much influence on my ancestors was Samuel Smart. He seems to have had a stroke of luck. He arrived in Freetown in 1826 from London (Pentonville) to practice law as a qualified attorney and solicitor. But the post of King's Advocate, who acted governor in a vacancy, a post normally only given to barristers, was vacant and as he was on spot he was appointed. He acted as governor twice (1826, 1828), his second term ending in a tussle with the officer commanding the troops who claimed a better right. He left in 1829 and subsequently practiced in Cape Colony and Australia, returning to London in 1853 (not therefore, one of the many victims of the "deadly miasma").

It is my assumption that Okoroafor, who by this time held a high respectable position amongst the Ibos and the Liberated Africans in general, was much involved with Governor Smart in matters relating to the resettlement. A high respect and trust existed between the two. It was within this scenario and interaction that Okoroafor adopted the surname Smart. Sometime between 1826 and 1828. I will now call him Weeks Okoroafor-Smart First.

Interestingly, the surname Okoroafor will disappear for at least two generations. Then the family surname became Smart or Weeks-Smart. It was my grandfather Francis, great grandson of Okoroafor (Smart First) who would resurrect the name Okoroafor, and the family name Weeks-Okrafor-Smart (note the change of the spelling of Okoroafor to Okrafor). A section will be devoted to Francis. An intellectual, philanthropist, builder, entrepreneur and social reformer. A truly wonderful man.

Over the years for some unknown reason our Ibo surname of Okorafor has gone from this original spelling to Okrafor-Smart and now Okrafo. Okoroafor must be differentiated from Okafor. Two different family names from different parts of what was Eastern Nigeria.

Smart First must have enjoyed a high status amongst the inhabitants of Regent, highly respected and loved. The 1831 census of Regent village shows that he had a four-acre property, that he was a carpenter (and must have therefore learnt his trade from Weeks). He had built himself a frame house (one of only fifteen in the village). He had two daughters living at home (his son by now living on his own). He had two male apprentices (which suggests that he was doing good business). His wife had two domestics, one a newly liberated girl, and kept poultry. When he died in 1837, four hundred people attended his funeral. Witness this account of his death by John Weeks.

> 'Yesterday about 8 o'clock the wife of John Smart (the person I baptised nine days ago) came to me with haste and said that her husband wished to see me before he departs, I went accordingly, he was very low then, he would not speak, save that he answered me these two questions. How do you feel now John Smart? He replied, I feel very well, for I

am going home to my Saviour and my God. Do you have any doubts in you mind about going home? "No", replied he. In addition to the answer to my question he said, "My sins are washed in the precious blood of Christ, the way is quite open for me, I shall soon go. The hour is quite near, when my pains shall cease". These and other sentences in faltering voice, I could not understand the rest before I left he spoke no more, he peacefully slept in the Lord Jesus Christ. I rejoiced greatly in the way he spoke. He felt no pain when he was speaking.

'The same evening I went over to Regent to perform the last ceremony over the mortal remains of one who left a good hope that he has entered into glory. More than 400 of the inhabitants attended his funeral'[5].

Missionaries travelling in West Africa

Thus ended the life of our ancestor the First Okoroafor-Smart who, according, to oral family history, arrived about 1816. He spent twenty-one years in Sierra Leone before he passed away. He was well respected.

John, his son, is likely to have been born before 1820, if he was senior enough to be village headman when he accompanied Reverend E N Jones on the Niger mission in 1853. According to our family tradition he was Weeks' first convert. It is also plain from the extract from Weeks' journal that his mother must have been converted before her husband died in 1837.

After John First died, John Second's wife gave birth to twins in 1841. Eventually John Second became headman, his comparative youth, one may assume, compensated for by his status as Weeks' early convert.

Over the next three generations the son of John First and his grandsons would play major roles in the Missionary Field and education in West Africa.

Oral family history indicates, that John First became very closely associated with John Weeks, the teacher, administrator and later Bishop of Sierra Leone, from 1855 to 1857. John Weeks would become very influential in the day to day life of John Second and his family.

Who was John Weeks? Where and when did he arrive in Sierra Leone? What was his role and how did he contribute in those early days in the establishment of our rural villages, education and the spread of Christianity.

Arrival in Freetown, Sierra Leone from Nigeria

APPROACH TO FREETOWN, CAPE LIGHT HOUSE, SIERRA LEONE

2

John Weeks 1800 - 1857

The British Modern Missionary Society movement emerged at the end of the 18th century and the beginning of the 19th century, as a major philanthropic enterprise. The object was global conversion. Men from ordinary parishes or circuits and with ordinary British backgrounds were the focus of recruitment efforts. It was not the social elite that were targeted by the Society. The justification given was the need for conversion of men and women. A further inducement was the implied hope for the missionaries of a rise in their worldly status.

The Church Missionary Society was established in Sierra Leone in 1804. Amongst those who came forward was John Weeks. John Weeks was born in St Petrox, Dartmouth, Devon, and baptised in the parish church in October 1800. As a young man he responded to the call to Labour in Sierra Leone, but why Sierra Leone?

Growing up in Dartmouth, it was possible that he might have been in touch and spoken to the sailors coming through from Sierra Leone. Dartmouth was a major port for collection of fresh food and water for ships on the way to the New World. Maybe he most probably must have spoken to sailors about the slave trade and the horrors and hardship experienced by the displaced Africans. Therefore his determination to go to Sierra Leone.

He was a successful carpenter and later trained as a school teacher. These two professions would in time be of immense value in Sierra Leone. On November 3rd 1824 he sailed for Sierra Leone, arriving in early 1825. Within a short time of his arrival, he was appointed as the Church Missionary Agent at Regent. Regent was an important District, a village about eight miles from Freetown. It was there the first Missionary Society Church, was built in 1816, St Charles'. He spent over twenty years in Sierra Leone, returning to England at various intervals. He was to become Bishop of Sierra Leone in1855.

Once he arrived in Sierra Leone he immersed himself not only in the strictly theological side of missionary work, but also in the more religio-cultural aspects.

Street Preaching, Freetown

This included education and more practical endeavours such as supervising the building of roads and bridges, as an aid to the advance of a civilised infrastructure. He also visited Liberated Africans as they arrived in Freetown.

Weeks' rapport with the Africans was significant, unlike other missionaries, his interaction with the Africans was one based in respect and understanding.

Soon after his arrival and once established in Regent, Weeks had a powerful impact on important people like Bishop Crowther and the Okafor-Smart family as a whole. His respect within that family resulted in the family adopting the name Weeks, subsequently passed down through their descendents.

Within twelve years of the arrival of John First the family name had taken a new labelling:

1816 – Okoroafor
1826-28 – Okoroafor-Smart (after Governor Smart)
1830's – Weeks Okrafor-Smart (after John Weeks)

Not only was the surname of Weeks added but the missionary's Christian name John had been adopted as well and passed down through the generations.

Interestingly, as if to emphasise the influence and respect Reverend John Weeks had with my ancestors, it is noted that even the names of his sisters left behind in Devon were passed on to those early descendants of John First. Names like Mary, the name of John Weeks' mother, Elizabeth, name of John Weeks' sister[6].

It was the usual practice for the early Liberated Africans to take on names of missionaries. The process itself was much more constructive, and was related to the funding of education in Sierra Leone. Varieties of fund-raising strategies were tried. One was a system whereby children rescued from slavery and resettled in Sierra Leone would be redeemed at, sum not exceeding £10 for each child. This plan was unsuccessful as there were moral issues. It looked as if they were being bought, and later abandoned[7].

Although the plan had come to an end, the missionaries were determined to turn the benevolence of their friends to good account by substituting some plan less open to objection. The CMS announced that they were ready to continue the plan at the rate of £5 per annum for each child. Each patron was to affix a name to each child for whom subscribed. This idea found many patrons in England and soon the CMS was able to report that £500 had been donated in 1813 towards the fund for maintaining and educating recaptured African children sent to Sierra Leone at £5 per annum. The children so provided for received the names of their benefactors. This system is mainly responsible for the large number of European family names borne by African Krios in Sierra Leone and was significant in the funding of education in the early days[8].

In May 1825, John Weeks was now settled as a teacher[9]. He was joined by his wife Anna in teaching, as was often the case with the missionaries. He informed CMS headquarters in London, in his journal of 25th March 1830 that attendance in the Regent School was 286, with an average daily attendance of 254. He now had ten regular teachers or monitors for different classes. Prior to this, there had always been lack of a suitable and sufficient supply of teachers. Now it was becoming possible to involve Africans as teachers or classroom helpers. He attributed the success to the additional instruction and remuneration given to the children[10].

Mrs. Weeks continued to support her husband and contributed hugely to the education of children in Regent in those early pioneering days of education of the resettled Africans. Unfortunately she died in January 1839 after 13 years of marriage to John Weeks. He remarried Mrs. Phoebe Graham in 1840. She died in Brixton, London, in 1866.

John Weeks' long survival in Sierra Leone with her history of being known as "The White Man's Grave" was unique. He first went out in 1825 and died in Sierra Leone in 1857. Although he made several visits to England between 1825 and 1845 he was absent for a period of just over 2 years. In 1846 he moved to London after his services to Sierra Leone of nearly 21 years. He became Vicar of St Thomas, Lambeth, from 1846 to 1855. In 1855 he became the Bishop of Sierra Leone, following Bishop Owen Emeric Vidal, DD (Doctor of Divinity), 1852 to 1854.

It is a real irony that John Weeks would become the Bishop because his request to take Holy Orders was refused,[11] the reason being he was thought to be "too worldly".

He was known as "The Friend of the Africans". Perhaps it was his love for the Africans that brought him into lasting friendship with my ancestors.

The missionaries tended to be suspicious of societies which often perpetuated old non-Christian practices and could be made an excuse for heavy drinking. But they came to realise that they could not break institutions so deeply rooted, and must therefore try instead to associate themselves with them and make them Christian companies, where dispute settling and other activities could still go on but under Christian regulations. For years Weeks struggled at Regent until in 1843 he succeeded. After six weeks hard negotiation, the leaders of the largest company agreed to submit their rules to him – and to show that they were doing it voluntarily, in a friendly spirit, they handed over an unexpected donation of £5 to CMS funds.

John Weeks died in 1857. His death was reported in The Gentleman's Magazine dated July 1857.

Bishop John Wills Weeks DD
1855-1857

Clergy Deceased

March 25th at Sierra Leone, the Right Reverend John William Weeks DD, Lord Bishop of Sierra Leone, having only returned on the 17th from visiting the stations of the Yoruba Mission of the Church Missionary Society. The "African" a Sierra Leone paper, of the 26th March gives the following account of the last moments of the departed Bishop:- "It is with a heavy heart that we have to announce to our readers the death of the Right Reverend Doctor Weeks, which took place about a quarter to five yesterday morning. The hopes that were entertained that a return to his own home and the love of friends might contribute to restore his shattered frame have proved vain. He gradually sank from the morning of his landing on the 17th inst, and yielded up his spirit in sure hope of seeing Him in whom he had believed. A most touching incident occurred a few hours before his death. He was asked by a friend, "Is the Lord precious to your soul?" A smile lit up the features that were already showing the effects of approaching dissolution, when he deliberately spelt the word "precious", pronouncing each letter distinctly, and then added "very". They were the last words which he was heard to speak, and soon after all that was before the eyes of weeping friends was but the cold and earthly tabernacle of the departed spirit. [12]

His career as a bishop, however short, was memorable. He had established a native ministry. Seven native catechists (including John Smart Second), who later went in the Niger Expedition (1853), were admitted by him to the deaconate in this colony and four in Abeokuta, Nigeria.

A dedication to the three first bishops of Sierra Leone; Right Reverend Owen Emeric Vidal DD 1852 to1854, Right Reverend John William Weeks DD 1855 to 1857 and Right Reverend John Bowen DD 1857 to 1860 could be seen at the east window in St George's Cathedral, Freetown.

Interior of St George's Cathedral, Freetown, Sierra Leone

Bishop Vidal was only fourteen months in actual residence in his diocese. Bishop Weeks was some two months longer. The one was struck down while young and full of life and hope; the other had been a veteran in his Master's Service and is laid in the midst of those to whom his name had been a household word. His grave can be seen next to that of the Smarts' family grave near the stream by the Cotton Tree at Regent. This is surely an indication of his strong connection with my ancestors. John Weeks married twice. His first wife was Mrs. Anna Pope in 1826; she died January 10th 1839. His second wife was Mrs. Phoebe Graham in 1840; she died in Brixton in 1866. There were no children from either marriage.

Much research has been done by the author on John Weeks, mainly because of his close connection with our ancestors. Oral history within the family portrayed different stories. One that was held for generations was the story of him ministering in Nigeria where he became friends with the local chief whose wife had given birth to twins. In those days it was a belief of the Ibo people that it is unnatural to produce more than one child at a time therefore one of the twins must be left in the forest to die. The story goes on to say that John Weeks quickly took the twins, brought them to Sierra Leone where they were adopted and baptised, given the names of Francis and Frederick Weeks Smart. That was their belief for a long time.

That was not the case. The twins were actually born in Sierra Leone at Regent in 1841. It is possible that John Weeks played an important part in their educational development because he was very close to their father John Smart Second who had been admitted as a catechist by John Weeks. It is also possible that the Ibo settlers in Regent had not given up their ancestral practice of discarding one of the twins at birth, therefore John Weeks had to rescue the boys.

Another important link between John Weeks and our ancestors are names given to our family.

These Christian names Mary, Elizabeth, Phoebe, John and William can be found in the family over the generations.

John Weeks' eldest sister was called Mary, so was his mother, baptised at St Petrox, Devon, in May 1787. Another sister Elizabeth Weeks was baptised at the same church in 1791. A brother, William Weeks was baptised in October 1793 and John Weeks himself in 1800. John is the most popular name and members of my family over the generations have been called John, an indication of the respect and love for John Weeks.

3

An Account of the early years of Regent by Christopher Fyfe[13].

Regent Church, the first stone church built in the colony of Sierra Leone.

Archaeologists may one day reveal whether the site of Regent village was inhabited before the nineteenth century. The first village to be sited there known from written records was founded in 1809. In that year Governor T. P. Thompson had a road cut, going down the eastern slope of Leicester Mountain as far as the stream, known as the Hogbrook, that flowed along the valley. He sent some recaptives, newly landed from slave ships, to live at the junction of road and stream, calling the settlement "Kingston-in-Africa" after his home town in England, Kingston-on-Hull. This settlement does not seem to have lasted.

The real foundation of the village was in July 1813 when a shipload of Vai people, captured off Cape Mesurado and freed by the Vice-Admiralty Court in Freetown which heard cases of slave-trading, were sent to settle by the Hogbrook. Other recaptives joined them and within a year there were over 500. They were under the care of Charles Shaw, one of the Maroon settlers from Jamaica where he had helped to organise the rebellion against the government for which the Maroons had been deported. In Sierra Leone he remained a leading figure in the community and was often employed on official duties.

Sir Charles MacCarthy, governor of Sierra Leone from 1814 to 1824, was determined to turn Regent and the other recaptive settlements that were being founded into well-organised villages. He wanted to see them laid out in an orderly fashion round a parish church where the people would be ministered to by missionaries and turned into Christians. In 1816 he wrote to the Secretary of State in London explaining his policy, and describing the village by the Hogbrook to which he had given the name of "Regent" after George, Prince of Wales, who was at that time acting as Prince Regent for his father George III. He reported that the village people were building a church – the first stone church to be opened in Sierra Leone. The construction was being supervised by a European army sergeant, but was carried out by them. It was named St Charles in honour of MacCarthy (who, though himself a Roman Catholic, founded Protestant churches all round the peninsula).

That same year, 1816, Regent was visited by the Secretary of the Church Missionary Society, Reverend Edward

Bickersteth, who had come out from London to inspect the mission. Fresh shiploads of recaptives had been regularly arriving, so that the population had by then risen to 1100. A Welsh Methodist teacher, Thomas Hirst, was in charge of them. At Bickersteth's recommendation, the CMS, with substantial financial support from the government, then took control of all the recaptive villages in the Colony.

A German missionary, William Augustine Johnson, was sent to Regent. He was to make the village famous. A dedicated missionary with a charismatic power of attracting people to him, he turned the recaptive villagers into a Christian community. To begin with he forced the people to go to church. He was a magistrate as well as a missionary and so could make them do what he wanted. Then they began going willingly, presumably seeing church-going as an integral part of the new life of freedom they were now leading.

Some of the stories about Johnson may have been exaggerated in the missionary propaganda publications that described his activities, but he unquestionably had a remarkable influence over his people. European visitors were amazed to find his church filled with an orderly congregation taking an intelligent part in the service. Some of them were made churchwardens. Soon the church was too small to hold everyone and had to be enlarged. Johnson saw to it that everyone in the village lived at least outwardly Christian lives. No one was allowed to work or make a noise on Sunday.

His journals describing his achievements in Regent were

sent to the CMS in London and extracts from them were published in CMS reports. They were to be a valuable resource for future mission publicists. A memoir of Johnson, filled with extracts from his journals, was published in London in 1853, followed by another version in abbreviated form for children, *Africa's Mountain Valley* by Maria Louisa Charlesworth, which sold thousands of copies. The frontispiece is an imaginary view of Regent showing church, mountain and stream.

MacCarthy loved to see buildings going up. At Regent a stone parsonage and school house were built and a stone-pillared market. He even had a house built there for himself. Streets were laid out in intersecting parallel lines on a grid pattern (in so far as the slope of the hillside allowed), and the intervening land divided into lots for the people to build houses on.

Many of the recaptives arrived from the slave ships in broken health, so a hospital was built. An African medical man was in charge, John Macaulay Wilson, son of the King of Kafu Bullom. He had been sent to England as a boy and trained as an apothecary, a profession that in those days combined the functions of druggist and doctor. On his return he entered government service, serving until 1828 when he succeeded his father as king. His reign was short: he only survived the initiation ceremonies by two weeks.

When Johnson left Regent in 1823, dying at sea on his way back to England, the population was over 2000. Most were Igbo from what is today Nigeria. After he had gone, church-going declined somewhat. Also some of MacCarthy's buildings, optimistically built on the hillsides, were washed away in the rains. Nevertheless the legacy of these two men survived. The Regent people had become quite different thanks to their efforts. Many had taken European names and were wearing European-style clothes. Most could speak English – some could read and write it. Many went regularly to church.

As Christians they were taught not to hide their talents but to work hard for themselves and put their earnings to good use. So they were ready to employ the new ways they had adopted in order to rise in the world. Farming only offered a good livelihood to a few, so the more enterprising would go down to Freetown to work. A survey made in 1826 showed that a hundred were working there regularly, some returning home every evening, some only once a week.

Peter Hughes was an outstanding figure among these early Regent villagers. One of Johnson's first communicants and church wardens, he soon learnt to read and write. A letter he wrote in 1819 to Johnson who was then on leave in London survives in the CMS archives. A stonemason by trade, he built himself a stone house in Regent. He also had a house in Freetown, in Goderich Street, where he and his wife Nancy carried on a successful butchery and meat contracting business. When Holy Trinity church was built in 1839 he was master-mason. He also supervised the rebuilding in 1855. Here, then, was a prosperous, self-made man, who had raised himself, as so many of his compatriots were then doing, by the associated ladders of business enterprise and religion.

In 1829 Regent witnessed one of those improbable coincidences that enliven the study of history. The CMS agent in charge of the village was John Weeks, an English schoolteacher of working-class origin, who was looked down on by some of his better educated fellow missionaries. His assistant was a young Yoruba receptive, Ajayi, who had taken the name Samuel Crowther. No one in 1829 would have dreamed that these two humble, obscure teachers, one white, one black, would both end their lives as bishops. Weeks served for twenty years in Sierra Leone, chiefly at Regent, and then moved to an impoverished parish in London. He returned in 1855 as second bishop of Sierra Leone and died after two years. Crowther, ordained in 1843, was in 1864 created Bishop of the Niger Territories, the first African bishop of the Church of England, officiating until his death in 1891.

A careful census of the Sierra Leone Colony was taken in 1831, the most reliable there has ever been. It showed 1766 people living in Regent, 1029 men, 737 women. Three men owned stone-built houses – Peter Hughes, and two CMS employees. Fifteen owned wooden framed houses. The rest had thatched houses of familiar style. Crowther lived in the schoolhouse with his wife and son (his other children were not yet born) and four receptives whom he was training. Another teacher, Edward Bickersteth, also shared the schoolhouse. Most of the people had by then taken English names, Macaulays predominating.

It was difficult for the CMS to recruit enough missionaries to staff all the villages. Government officials called managers were put in instead. But the villagers had no need for a government agent to rule them. They were perfectly able to preserve law and order themselves; a manager had so little to do in the Mountain villages (which included Regent) that the post was given up in 1855. In Regent and the other villages the people formed "companies", usually consisting of those from the same homeland (Yoruba, Igbo, Congo, etc), or occupational, like the hunters, in which the elected office-bearers kept the peace among the members. Disputes that concerned more than one group were referred to the "Seventeen Nations" which represented them all. So Regent was a quiet, orderly village. The people had their own institutions of government, settled their own disputes, and were not ordered about by outsiders.

Regent becoming established both spiritually and socially unified.

Weeks' successor, Reverend Nathaniel Denton, also induced all church members to join a "Church Company" in addition to their existing companies. So the church was an important focus of village life, as MacCarthy had intended it should be. A Methodist church was also opened in about 1840. By then all the village people were at least nominally Christians and attended church and class. No one openly followed non-Christian worship. When the church buildings needed repair or rebuilding, as they often did, they did the work themselves.

In 1856 they had the pleasure of seeing one of their own sons officiating there, Reverend George Crowley Nicol. Born in Regent in 1823 (though his father Pompey Nicol, a recaptive

Temne Sawyer, moved the following year to Gloucester), Nicol was educated in England by the CMS and ordained in 1849. He married Susan Crowther, one of the bishop's daughters. When, in 1861, the CMS gave up control of most of the village parishes and a Native Pastorate took over, he became the first pastor of Regent. Later he held the post of Colonial Chaplain in the Gambia, and died in 1907.

Some recaptives and their children still longed for their distant homelands. Others, less sentimental, nevertheless saw that the small Sierra Leone Colony offered only limited scope for enterprise and sought better opportunities elsewhere. Emigration to the Yoruba country began in 1839. In 1853 a party of Igbo, including John Smart, headman of Regent, went to look for prospects in their land of origin. When the CMS opened a Niger Mission under Crowther's supervision, he and two other Regent men, Thomas John and Alexander Day, were employed as their agents.

John Smart had charge of the CMS station at Onitsha. His son, Reverend Frederick Weeks Smart followed him to the Niger Mission, resigning from the CMS in 1876. On return to Freetown he opened a high school in Freetown in Pademba Road, moving eventually to Accra as headmaster of the government school, and dying there in 1888. His twin brother Francis was in charge of the government school on the Isles de Los until it was closed in 1894. Another unrelated Regent Smart, Reverend Simeon Smart, also served in the Niger Mission, returning to Sierra Leone to officiate in various parishes and, on retirement, going home to Regent where he died in 1907.

Thus from Regent, as from the other villages, enterprising sons and daughters tended to move away along the coast to seek their fortunes abroad – returning perhaps in old age to rest their bones in their quiet birthplace. One of Regent's most distinguished descendants, Dr. John Randle (1855 to 1928), a medical practitioner in Lagos, endowed a charity to relieve the poor of the village.

Since MacCarthy's days Regent has delighted European visitors, some of whom described it in books. F. Harrison Rankin, who was for a short while in government service in Sierra Leone in the early 1830s, visited it and described its beautiful setting in his book *The White Man's Grave,* published in 1836. He was impressed – not altogether favourably – by the independent-minded way the villagers received him: instead of showing him respect as a white man, they seemed to regard him as an intruder on the privacy of their home. Reverend T.E. Poole, Colonial Chaplain, also commented on the beauty of Regent in his *Life, Scenery and Customs in Sierra Leone* (1850). On his visit he lodged comfortably with an elderly villager, Mr. Thomas, who was ready to let his well furnished house to visitors.

Regent was also depicted, very favourably, by the traveller Winwood Reade in *The African Sketchbook* (1873). He stayed there for a while and became acquainted with pastor Nicol whom he esteemed highly. His book, an eccentric mixture of short stories and valuable descriptive information, contains a story entitled "The Pastor's Daughter" which is partly set in Regent. It is an imaginary tale about the daughter of an African pastor (not Nicol) who falls in love with a British army officer. When she hears he is going to marry a European lady she falls ill and dies! In real life, however, a different story can be told. Major W. J. Ross, a British army officer, when he retired from army service, settled down at Regent. There he met and married a young lady, Hannah Campbell, and lived there for forty-one years, dying in 1912 at the age of eighty-one.

Regent and the other villages declined in size as its inhabitants moved away. By the 1890s the population had fallen to about one thousand. But Temne and other farmers moved in as tenants (for the property owners kept possession of their land) to keep up the numbers, since the fertile soil always provided a livelihood for market gardeners. So it was less of a "deserted village" than some of the more outlying places. When the centenary celebrations were held in 1913, though its more flourishing days were long past, the village people could still pride themselves on maintaining a peaceful, law-abiding community in the beautiful setting of the wooded mountains.

4

John Smart Second

As had been mentioned earlier John Smart Second was, according to family history, John Weeks' first convert.

He would become headman of Regent village. He attained such a high position presumably because his late father John First was highly respected and held in very high esteem. Remember that his funeral in 1837 was attended by over four hundred people.

If John Smart Second was born immediately his father arrived in Freetown, we believe in about 1816, he would have been eight years of age when John Weeks arrived in Freetown from Devonshire.

His early schooling could have been under John Weeks and then progressed from the primary school at Regent to the Mission school. He then became Headman of Regent.

He must have been a busy person fulfilling his duties as an administrator, being the headman of Regent. Administrating village activities such as being involved in settling disputes, which would have arisen in view of the various ethnic mix of the village. John would be the representative as participant to official engagements, meeting important visitors and, of course the spokesman, putting forward ideas for the development and improvements within the village of Regent. His most impressive commitment was accompanying the Reverend E Jones on the Niger Mission of 1853.

Witness a statement by Reverend E Jones regarding John Smart.

'In consequence of several letters addressed to the local committee by the leading men of the Ibo tribe most of whom were not in connection with us, as well as of an application from John Smart of Regent one of our oldest communicants in that station, praying us to send them back to their own country, that they might see if the way was open to send the gospel to their country people'. Reverend E Jones continued.

'I was directed by the local committee to take three persons with me, John Smart of Regent, Jacob Cole, an intelligent schoolmaster from Waterloo, and his father who were all Ibos and see if it were possible to reach the Ibo country'[14].

Reverend Jones and his party left Freetown in April 1853 and returned in June of the same year.

On his return the results of his mission was published as follows:

'It should however be noted that the delegation did not reach the Niger. By the time the boat had taken them to Fernando-Po, Jones said he was (1) Fully satisfied in (his) mind from conversations with naval officers and others that it would not be possible for them to ascend the Niger and reach Aboli (South of Onitsha) unless in a steamer; (2) That the way by Bonny is still less so from the treacherous character of the people; (3) That any members of Christian Ibos or Calabars might safely settle on the Calabar river where our Scottish brethren would welcome them. That Fernando-Po from its situation offers peculiar facilities as a baseline for future missionary operations in the great rivers of the Gulf of Guinea'. He concluded, 'May the Lord direct the Parent Committee to a right judgement'[15].

John Smart Second thus returned to Regent where he continued his official capacity as the villagers headman.

John Smart Second went back to Nigeria. This time as a Catechist with the Niger Mission and served for a year 1858 to 1859, based in Onitsha, Nigeria[16]. As was the practice, his journals were sent to the mission headquarters in London quarterly.

Nigeria – Niger Mission 1857-1882

CA 3036

Original Papers – Letters and Papers of individual missionaries and catechists

John Smart 1858-1859

Text of sermon preached by John Smart, Onitsha, Nigeria, 19th December 1858, whilst serving as a catechist in the Niger Mission 1858 to 1859.

Matthew 25 v15

'And unto one he gave five talents to another two and to another one. To everyman according to his several ability'.

From another sermon on 6th February, 1859 his text was from John 11 v24.

'Jesus said unite – I am the resurrection and the life, he that beliveth in me though he was dead, yet shall he live'.[17]

Why was his time in Onitsha so brief?

Unfortunately, there seems to be an abrupt end. One can only conclude that as with the early missionaries he probably passed away. If so, was he buried in Nigeria from where his father came to Sierra Leone in about 1816?

What is known was that he had some children, amongst whom were the twins Francis and Frederick, who were born in Regent in 1841. Further research into family history convinced me that the twins might have had two sisters at least.

As could be expected of the children of the headman of Regent, who was also strongly linked to the church, they should by right have had a good education. Witness the educational development of twins Frederick and Francis. They had a good pedigree for participating in the Christianising and civilising mission in West Africa. To be successful in such a field meant having a good education. Both started school at the infants then primary schools in Regent.

5

Frederick Weeks-Smart 1841 - 1888

Frederick entered the grammar school in Freetown on June First 1860. His enrolment number being 856 in the register. He did very well at primary school before going to the grammar school. On completion, went on to Fourah Bay College. In 1868 he was

Old Fourah Bay College

appointed a catechist to the Niger Mission and was stationed in Bonny, Nigeria. He was subsequently ordained in 1871. In 1870 he had compiled a PRIMER in the Ibo language and also translated a few hymns. From 1871 he was in charge of St Stephen's Church in Bonny. His quarterly reports were sent to the Missionary headquarters in London. These reports gave an insight into his activities in relation to his missionary work. Looking back and reading these archival documents creates a vivid picture of the social history and his world. The objectives of the Niger Missions were broadly speaking to introduce the Gospel and the elements of a Christian civilisation.

Frederick's quarterly journals were sent regularly to the CMS Mission Headquarters in London. In his journal for the year ending September 30th 1872 he wrote: "After spending six pleasantest and happiest months with my fond relatives and friends at home (i.e. Sierra Leone – Regent), during which period it was my greatest pleasure and happiness to take to myself a dear partner in life. After making all preliminary arrangements to return to the scene of my missionary labours, I embarked this evening with my dear wife on board the SS 'Congo' amidst the affectionate adieus and blessings of our friends and relatives. Separation was indeed keenly felt on both sides. But nevertheless we 'conferred not with flesh and blood, and our friends entirely agreed with us that in advancing the Gospel of Christ, no preparation should be too painful, and no sacrifice made by us …..'[18].

A Comment by Christopher Fyfe

Bonny (in today's Nigeria) where Frederick was stationed was an ancient kingdom where people had been trading peaceably with Europeans for about three hundred years. In the early years it had been trade in slaves but by this time it was trade in palm oil. It was an orderly, well-governed place with a small settled community of European merchants. The missionaries could live there under the protection of the government without any danger. Though Frederick mentions a civil war they were in no way personally affected by it.

The mission was newly established and was staffed by African missionaries. The European missionary who came out with him (Mr. Comber) died almost at once, leaving Sierra Leoneans in charge. It seems to have been well organised, supervised by Reverend Dandeson Crowther, eldest son of Bishop Crowther, an efficient and helpful leader who could supervise the building of a substantial church as well as managing the pastoral duties. Reading through the journals I felt Frederick was a man carrying out his duties with enjoyment, in not uncongenial surroundings, work he was ideally suited for and did very well.

Nigeria – Niger Mission
1857-1882

CA 3035

Original Papers – Letter and Papers of individual missionaries and catechists

Rev. Frederick Weeks-Smart
1868-1880

Introduction to Journals

The journals of Frederick Smart sent every quarter to the CMS (Church Missionary Society) in London gave a true picture of the social history of the Ibo people in particular during his time of Ministry in the Bonny Region. The Niger Mission, 1868 to 1876.

As with other Missionaries his main vision was conversion at any costs. That was the basic objective. Closely followed by education and the spread of Christianity. Success in these areas would create the basis for a Christian family. The accomplishment/success in these areas, i.e. conversion and the establishment of the family unit, would be the greatest challenge missionaries like Frederick faced living amongst the Ibos who practised polygamy and the worship of idols. These are central to their national beliefs. Frederick, however, had an advantage compared with his fellow missionaries. This being that he could speak the native tongue. He produced a Primer in the Ibo language and this was widely used in the schools.

His acceptance and success would be measured by the number of converts he accounted for, and he was always quoting the number of worshippers in his Sunday service, both morning and evening. For example on a particular Sunday 400 people were at service in the morning and 150 people were at service in the evening. Very high numbers. This illustrated a changing time in their beliefs and eagerness towards conversion.

His journals on many occasions gave accounts of people coming to the Mission House with their Juju, these to be destroyed.

It is important to note that it was not all success because not all of the chiefs were convinced or won over towards the acceptance of the Christian faith. Those that did were totally immersed and easily abandoned their native evil practices. It is noted that, in some cases, the chiefs would offer their premises and invite local people to assemble in order to hear Frederick preach and talk about the benefits of doing away with the practice of Juju (idolatry).

As far as one can assess the journals did not inform us as to whether they went back to their heathen ways once they'd become converted. A point of interest is the observation that in some cases the converts would adopt the names of the Missionary who converted them. These names would then be passed on from father to son or daughter – surnames such as Benn, Macauley, Thomas etc.

Also important to note was the fact that in some cases it would be the children once converted who would get their parents drawn to the Christian way.

In his journal of September 1873 he gave an account of domestic slavery and wrote about the inhumanity of such evil practices and paid tributes to the philanthropists, who worked for the Abolition of Slavery, and the work being done by David Livingstone.

In the journal of November 1873 he gave an account of a service he conducted on the day before troops set out to fight in the Ashanti Expedition. Because of its historical significance this journal was sent to Mr. Christopher Fyfe the archivist and historian. His comments are attached.

His journal of 15th May 1876 illustrated the sad event of the passing away of his first wife. This I found very moving indeed. Sadly, he would resign from the Mission due to circumstances in relation to his wife's illness and subsequent death.

Bonny Mission
Journal for the quarter ending September 1868
Introduction

After completing my course of study in the Society's College at Fourah Bay, Sierra Leone, together with two of my fellow students, the Local Committee upon the application of Bishop Crowther appointed me to Bonny Mission in the capacity of Catechist. Accordingly having no time, I made the necessary arrangement and preparation for embarkation which took place on the 9th April 1868.

Our party consisted of the late Reverend Mr. Comber and Mrs. Comber with whom I was to labour at Bonny. Mr. & Mrs. John Charles Moore, who were destined to the newly taken up Brass Mission, and myself.

After a voyage of 13 days we safely arrived at our destination, where we were joyfully welcomed by the Bishop (Edward Beckles, Bishop of Sierra Leone 1860-1870) and all the Mission Agents. We were not however, a full day in this new sphere of Labour, when, to our utmost surprise and disappointment not to say grief, one of our party, the Reverend Mr. Comber was suddenly attacked by mental derangement. The painful sensation which this sad event excited, was much more enhanced by the fact that no proper medical attendance was at command. Though every care and means in our power was used, yet the malady continued to increase and assume more dangerous features. At length the poor servant of God succumbed under it, and expired in the arms of his Saviour whom he so ardently loved, and for whose causes he had willingly forsaken a dear mother and sister at home.

This afflictive dispensation took place on the 7th May, just a fortnight after our arrival.

The remains were interred on the following morning. The ceremony was performed by the Bishop.

The Journal continues:-

The day is remarkable as being that on which the most influential chiefs came to our agreement among themselves and had it drawn up in a document that <u>they would never for the future maintain the inhuman practice of destroying or exposing to death their twin infants</u>. Chief Maximillan Pepple alias William Banjo was the leading man in this noble transaction. This was a result of a sermon preached before them by the Bishop in the residence of the king on the subject, which sermon made such impression on their minds as to influence them to this measure. Indeed the <u>word of the Lord is great and powerful</u>.

17th on yam harvesting.

Offering made to juju. The next seven days were spent celebrating the feast, which consists chiefly in making sacrifices, drinking, singing, drumming and dancing.

Brother Carew and myself went this afternoon to witness the ceremonies. We observed a high priest together with four or five priests in the juju temple erected under a thick grove very near to the Mission House and Church.

There was an <u>outer court</u> under the open sky. Here all the people were assembled waiting for the priest to call them in and do the rites for them. There was an <u>inner court</u> for the priests.

He then went on to say...

It is gratifying to remark that our school children did not join in these heathen festivities nor did they comply when they were demanded by their country people to eat the offerings made of juju. Some of them suffered domestic persecution in consequence.

23rd

Visited an old sick woman. Her hut was very miserable – dark, damp and narrow. She was lying near a fire on a single board placed on the ground. I showed her the way and the only way too to eternal life. Exhorted her to take a firm grasp of Jesus by faith in her Saviour and Redeemer. She was very much inspired and thanked me for coming to visit her.

2nd August 1868

The Lord's Day. The services of the day were interesting. The attendance was satisfactory,

Chief Jack William Pepple permitted his wives to attend church today.

16th August 1869

Was informed this morning that the sick woman whom I used to visit died last night. The juju priests performed the funeral ceremonies. Went to town in the afternoon and had religious conversation with some of the chiefs.

20th August 1868

Had street preaching in the town this morning as well as domiciliary visitation.

Conclusion of Journal

In concluding my journal for the quarter. I have great pleasure to remark that the progress of our work is slow but sure. We are laying foundation upon which to work afterwards.

A great ground is daily growing upon the kingdom of Satan as it exists here, but yet little or nothing is observed concerning this. "Faith, yet pursuing is, however, our motto let us not despise the day of small things, but let us with faith, continue in the work of the Lord having this one assurance we "shall reap if we faint not".

Frederick Weeks Smart
CMS Catechist in
charge of Mission

Bonny Mission

Journal for the Quarter Ending September 1869

In presenting a journal of the details of my missionary labours during the quarter just come to a close, I would beg to express my deep regret that during the period under review very little of active work has on the whole been accomplished.

There has occurred, during the year, a succession of disastrous events in this country over which we could exercise no control, constantly keeping the popular mind in a state of excitement and painful apprehension. In April a most <u>calamitous</u> fire took place. In June, July and August the small-pox made its appearance and in September a dreadful Civil war broke out.

Under such painful and distracting circumstance therefore our school work and open air preaching in particular were suspended and our usual operation in general interrupted.

Nor does this discouraging state of things cease to exist. Up to this very moment in which I am writing, matters continue as they were; nor is there any present indication of their assuming a change for the better for several months to come.

But though discouraged, we have not been in despair. On the contrary, I am firmly persuaded that all these obstacles which have occurred to hinder, will sooner or later fall out rather unto the furtherance of the Gospel. Indeed as far as my own private feelings go, I am really full of hope and confidence for the future, and I sincerely trust that, within no distant day our work shall advance with far greater freedom and speed, than ever it had done may the God of Missions hasten this in his time!

I will now proceed to state, in a brief manner, some interesting particulars of what has taken place, and what opportunities of usefulness I have availed myself of during this quarter.

July 3rd

A bright sunny day this! I was engaged all the day in attending to the carpenters who were at work in Mrs. Samuels apartment.

In the evening I paid a visit to the Juju chief-priest at the village Iwammah in our immediate neighbourhood and entered into a long but interesting conversation with him on the subject of their mythology. He acknowledged that there exists one Supreme Being.

July 4th

The Lord's Day and a very wet day. Commenced Divine Service at half past ten o'clock. Spoke on Luke XVI 13. There seemed to be some impression made on the minds of the receivers as after the service about twelve men came to me and desired their names to be put down as inquirers, as they felt a strong influence on their minds to decide in favour of Jesus and his service with much hesitation I acceded to their request as fearing it is the effect of their excitement than of calm deliberation and decision. Time however will test their sincerity. Conducted the evening service and spoke on Exodus XXXII 26.

On the whole the attendance today was very good. There being present 52 of the natives in the morning and 102 in the evening.

August 1st

The Lord's Day Divine Service commenced at half past ten as usual this morning. I addressed the people on Genesis XV 1. Later walked over to Iwammah after service and had house to house visitation. At half past three in the afternoon I proceeded to the town, where I was happy to find a large number of persons sitting idly in the market place; an opportunity which I readily availed myself of, to make known the message of a Crucified Redeemer. Having closed my preaching here, I proceeded to the houses of some of the chiefs and held religious conversation with them. Returned home at about half past six in the evening, full of inward joy that the Lord had enabled me to sow some seed today in his Gospel vineyard. May some of the seeds at least thus scattered be so abundantly wakened by God the Holy Spirit without whose gracious aid, all our efforts will be in vain that souls may be saved and God glorified.

Bonny Mission
Journal for the year ending September 30th 1872

November 1871

After spending six pleasantest and happiest months with my fond relatives and friends at home (i.e. Sierra Leone), during which period it was my greatest delight and happiness to take to myself a dear partner in life, and after making all preliminary arrangements to return to due scene of my missionary labours, I embarked this evening with my dear wife on board the S S 'Congo' amidst the affecting and affectionate adieus and blessings of our friends. The separation was indeed keenly felt on both sides. But nevertheless we "conferred not with flesh and blood", and our friends entirely agreed with us that, in advancing the cause of Christ, no separation should be deemed too painful, and no sacrifice too dear. We all were under the full persuasion that the sacrifice made by us will be a cheap one indeed, if, by means of it, the morally dark and desolate wilderness of Bonny shall begin, in the smallest measure, to enjoy the blessed light of the gospel as well as the "rejoice and blossom as the rose".

November 2nd

In vain did we strain all the powers of vision this morning to catch if possible, one final glimpse of our native land. No evidence of any solitary object that spoke of home could be traced. All that appeared to view outside our limited abodes, whichever directions we turned were merely the wide expansion of the mighty Altantic below, and the spacious canopy of the lofty heavens above us. Then it was, that we entered into the full impact of the expression – "we have forsaken all".

November 9*th* 1871

Came to anchor off Lagos this morning, and went on shore where we were welcomed most cordially by our kind friends. Upon inquiry we soon learnt that the steamers that ascended the River Niger during the year were disastrously situated that it was impossible for them to effect their descent earlier than the next rainy season, and that, in consequence of this, our good Bishop and party would be under the necessity of returning home by an overland and tedious route which will require the period of more than a month to perform. A sad circumstance indeed! But who knows what beneficial results may follow out of this apparently untoward dispensation of providence? May God overrule all these mishaps to the advancement of his cause and the glory of his name.

At this place my wife was taken ill, and we were detained in consequence, much longer than we originally intended.

December 6*th*

Finding Mrs. Smart much improved in health, and thinking it sufficiently safe to proceed with her on the remaining part of our voyage, I took leave of our Lagos friends, this morning, and went with her on board the steamship 'McGregor Laird' for Bonny.

December 8*th*

Through the tender mercy and protecting hand of God, we safely arrived at our destination about 6 o'clock this evening, having had a very prosperous and speedy passage. We landed at night at the Mission Station where we met all the members of the Mission waiting to welcome us. We retired to rest with feelings of deep gratitude, to our heavenly Father for the "goodness and mercy" that had followed us since we left Sierra Leone.

9th December

The news of our arrival having spread like wild fire all over the town and villages, the natives came pouring into my house this morning, and during the course of the day, to greet my return. Great was the joy they expressed at seeing Mrs. Smart whom they welcomed into their country with every visible and pleasing demonstration of goodwill and esteem. In view of these cheering circumstances, we indeed "thanked God and took courage".

December 10th

Lord's Day, Divine Service was held at half past ten o'clock this morning. Prayers were read by the Reverend D C Crowther and a discourse was given by myself to a very crowded and attentive audience text Luke XXIV 47. In the evening I read prayers and Reverend Crowther preached. The day was pleasantly, and I trust profitably spent. "How sweet a Sabbath this to spend in hopes of one that ne'er shall end."

Christmas Day 1871

A bright and charming morning. Up early and went out with some of the school boys to the bush to gather ever-greens with which to decorate little Bethel. Returned in time and performed work of decoration, the Reverend D C Crowther heartily co-operating with me. The whole place then assumed cheerful, brilliant, refreshing aspect. After this pleasing business was got through, we betook ourselves to our houses to hold ourselves in readiness for public worship.

The bell was rung at half past ten o'clock and Divine Service was commenced at eleven. After prayers which I read, Mr. Crowther gave a very beautiful discourse from the appropriate text of Matthew II 2. The place of worship was completely thronged. All the natives were in their best. The school children appeared of tidy hair cleanly, and sang with cheerful and pleasant voice. Every face was radiant with joy and they were eager to hear about the birth of the holy child.

Oh, it was a scene it would do any good to witness! As regards myself, I felt when I witnessed it, exceedingly animated and refreshed. It gave me great cause to hope that our feeble efforts to evangelize, and, by consequence, civilize these people but a few years ago were notorious cannibals and savages, will not be in vain. In fact, it maybe very sanguine in the future.

After the close of the service, numbers of the people came to wish us "a merry Christmas", all whom we received with kindness. In the afternoon a game of croquet was played on one side, at which the Mission party played with interest and gratification, and a foot-race on the other side at which the school children exercised themselves with the usual gusto. Every thing went off admirably, and the sun sank below the horizon leaving us profoundly thankful for the opportunity granted us to spend one more Christmas in this benighted land, in so pleasant a manner.

December 31st

May the Lord enable me by His Spirit to "redeem the time" which now lies before me, by availing myself more *diligently than ever, of every opportunity of "preaching the word" and winning souls to Christ. Conducted Divine Service worship this morning and preached to a very numerous and attentive congregation from the latter part of the 9th verse of the 90th Psalm.*

In the evening I read prayers and Mr. Crowther preached from Revelations III 20. May the precious seed of the gospel sown during the entire course of the year that is now closing upon us be abundantly watered from on high, that it may germinate, take root downward, and bear fruit upward, hundred fold, to the glory of Gods Holy Name!

January 1st 1872 - New Years Day

Today we were happily engaged in opening for public worship, a new Mission Church erected under the superintendence of the Rev. D C Crowther, during the later part of the past year. It is built on the site of the former mud-walled, bamboo-thatched school-chapel which served us hitherto as a place of worship, and as a school room.

It is in dimension of 56 by 30 ft. and is raised 2½ feet from the ground. It is made of durable boards, with five windows opening in opposite directions. The floor is paved with bricked and the roof covered with sheets of galvanised iron. The whole building is capable of holding 500 persons.

We began Divine Service within its walls at eleven o'clock this morning. After prayers which I read, Mr. Crowther preached to a large and interested audience.

May many of those for whose spiritual welfare this church was erected find that "lively the Lord is in this place;

and that this is none other but the house of God, and this is the gate of heaven!"

January 7th 1872

Lord's Day – Preached this morning from the words of Joshua – "Choose ye this day whom ye will serve." In the afternoon just about the time for Sunday School, an incident occurred, the recital of which will, I doubt not, deeply interest the feelings of the friends of Missions.

While I was in my study, Mrs. Smart heard a considerable noise out-of-doors, and came to inform me of it. On going out to see what was the cause of the noise, I was not a little agreeably surprised to see several boys bearing towards my house bundles of rubbish, followed by a small procession of other children, all shouting at the top of their voices Juju! Juju! Juju! When they came sufficiently near the door of my house, they threw down the bundles, and one of them informed me that they received order from his father to remove this rubbish out of this premises and to bring it to me. The rubbish consisted of a large number of the skulls, bones and horns of a variety of domestic and wild animals killed, perhaps, in sacrifice to the demon or demons out of whose shrines the rubbish was removed.

They were covered with dust and soot, which showed they were deposited within the shrines many years ago. All of the others in the Mission were soon gathered at the spot wondering at the curious spectacle and rejoicing at the extraordinary occurrences. It was not without some doubts that we should bring ourselves to believe the boys; the information or intelligence being as we surmised too gratifying to be credible. That Chief Oke Epella, a man well known as a *staunch votary of Jujuism would abandon this national system of false religion in so voluntary and public a manner, was an idea we thought it premature reasonably to entertain to place the matter beyond all reasonable doubts therefore, I hastened to the village Ayambo, where the chief is resident, to obtain an accurate knowledge of the real circumstances of the case. Arriving there in about half an hours time I found that, in fact, the fetish huts outside as well as within the chief's compound, had all been demolished. On entering his apartment, I was respectfully received by him. A friendly conversation then ensued in the course of which I introduce the subject thus:*

"Well Oke, I am extremely glad for what you have done today". He then asked, "What thing I do?" I replied, "You have thrown away your Juju and your boys have taken them over to me". He said, "Yes, it be me tell them to clear him up. I no want him again – I'm done with them things".

I then asked him his reasons for this line of conduct. His words in reply were these "Because he be nothing; he no fit (i.e. it cannot) do anything for me. That be may (i.e. why) I throw him away. And not be him make me too; it be God, make me. And it be me keep him for house, not be him keep me. And now I done hear God work, – my boy tell me too – it been thing make I try to believe God one time (i.e. it is the thing that caused me to try to believe God at once). That be the reason I throw them Juju away today". I then asked, "Are you sure you are not going to set up some new Juju in place of the old one you have now thrown away?" He replied – "I want make young (i.e. new) new, I no fit throw old me away" I then said "You are quite right I merely asked to because it wont be well to throw Juju away today,, and take it up again tomorrow." "That be true," he replied. "It no be proper to do that and I no fit do so too, not be man force me to throw him away, Poso man (Juju man) force me, then I must take him back. But it be myself like to throw him away. I no fit take him again. I no want him anymore!"

Upon this I asked, "What then will you do with your tai?" The tai is a family altar made of earth, dedicated to the household demon or demons, and erected in a corner of the entrance-room of every principal house in this place. He, in reply, said he would also break it down tomorrow as he did not wish any work to be done in God's holy day.

I assured him this kind of work could be done today. So he called out one of his men to break down the altar. The altar was accordingly dragged back to the ground, and the earth thrown out of the doors. Thus done the chief gave further orders and all the interior apartments of the entire house were thoroughly ransacked and every remaining fetish or charm was brought out and delivered up to me. After this I caused the 44th chapter of Isaiah, 6-20, to be read, by, the chief's son in the hearing of all, which passage I made a running commentary of, in the Eboe tongue, and closed the proceeding with prayer.

The fetishes and charms were all taken over to the Mission Station, where I arrived just in time to conduct the evening service. My discourse this evening was based upon the words "As for me and my house, we will serve the Lord." Joshua XXIV 15.

I must not omit to say that the chief was induced to abandon his gods by his son, a boy of about 13 years of age who is a constant attendant at the Mission School. This boy heard me preach this morning, and took home to this father what he heard. The father was so impressed with the simple truths thus unfolded, that he resolved at once to choose the worship of

Jehovah. A striking instance this, of the powerful influence under God our day-school is bringing to bear upon the adult population at home!

The events of this day are remarkable when we remember that since we established a Mission in this country, no chief had made such a public renunciation of the popular system of idolatry, as Chief Oko Epella has this day done. O God of Missions, grant that the other chiefs in this benighted.... Lord may also turn these vanities, unto thee, the Living God.

"Say to these chieftains from thy throne I am Jehovah, God alone!"

Thy voice therein idols shall compound and cast therein after to the ground.

January 13th 1872

Paid a visit to Chief Ibo Epella almost every evening during the course of this week to strengthen him with the word of God. At this time of the religious transition which he has entered upon, he surely needs careful and unremitting attention that he may retain his impressions and persevere in his enquiry after truth. Indeed at times of crisis of his religious history, it is highly important that he should be frequently nourished with the sincere milk of the word, that he may grow thereby.

January 17th

Went to Bonny town and held religious conversation with several of the chiefs returned to the Mission Station at sunset.

23rd January - Former Slave Market

In the afternoon we walked over to a small hamlet (Mrs. Smart and I) in the neighbourhood, the former scene of a slave market and baracoon. At this place there is a small beautiful lagoon where the slaves, we were informed, used to lay at anchor while they quietly surreptitiously stored and were hidden, so as to evade the detection of British cruisers. With the exception of certain fruit trees which told that the spot was once the seat of a civilised community nothing was left to distinguish the hamlet from the surrounding places. This awakened in me deep feelings of thankfulness to that gracious Provider who successfully enable William Wilberforce, Granville Sharp, Sir Thomas Fowell Buxton and other British philanthropists to give a coup-de-grace to this nefarious traffic on our West Coast. May the recent explorations of Dr. Livingstone tend to effect the same noble result on the East Coast.

After spending a very pleasant day, we took leave of our friends at Juju town and returned to the Mission Station where we safely arrived at night fall.

23rd February 1872

Took a short trip with Mrs. Smart to Juju town, a village a few miles down the river, on a visit to a kind chief by name Jack Brown. A canoe manned by twenty paddlers was kindly sent by the chief to carry us thither. We landed there in less than an hour's time, and met with a warm and cordial reception. After a hearty breakfast, I requested the chief to assemble his household, which he readily did. I then addressed all present on the subject of religion, laying particular stress on the proper observance of the Sabbath, which I have reason to believe was by no means generally thought of here. This address, I am happy to state, was not lost upon my hearers. For all felt that they ought to "remember the Sabbath day to keep it holy," and the chief himself made a promise, in the presence of his household, that he would from henceforth refrain from causing his men to work on this day of sacred rest. His son William who has spent two years in England was also in attendance, and assisted to explain to his father the advantages that will accrue to him if he pursued the course recommended. This young man is endeavouring to instruct a private school at his father's residence, and to bring his influence to bear favourably upon the people of that village generally. I consequently encouraged him to persevere in his efforts of usefulness.

March 29th

Good Friday. Conducted Divine Service at eleven o'clock this morning and preached from the words "we preach Christ crucified" First Corinthians Chapter 1 v 23. The number of hearers was 143. A deep impression seemed to be made on all present while the solemn and affecting story of the cross was being told.

31st Easter Day 1872

Had very interesting services, the number of person present in the morning was 216, and in the evening 143. The texts were Luke XXIV 34 and John XX 19. The Sunday School was attended by 110 scholars.

May 11th 1872

Brothers Johnson of Brass and During of Akassa, arrived here this morning per SS "Kwerra" from their respective stations. Mrs. Johnstone also accompanied them.

May 13th

A Clerical Conference was opened today by the Bishop. There were present the Reverends W Morgan, J White, D L Crowther, J Johnson, J During, Mr. Carew, the catechist and myself.

Many important subjects were brought forward for consultation and discussion all bearing upon the one absorbing question – what are the best ways and means of carrying on successfully the great work we have in hand? The brethren were all called upon to state their several missionary experiences for mutual counsel, encouragement and edification.

15th May 1872

The Conference came to a close today, such a Conference if held yearly at least would I am sure prove a source of considerable strength and affectiveness to the working of the entire Niger Mission.

For the able and fatherly manner all the proceedings were presided over by our excellent Bishop. We could not help feeling exceedingly thankful to Almighty God, for placing over us so judicious, devoted and experienced a personage. May he be long spared to be an ornament to the Episcopal Choir of the Niger Territory of which he is the first occupant.

Frederick's Ordination by Bishop Crowther

May 26th 1872

Trinity Sunday – A memorable day this, in the history of the Mission. The services this day were the most solemn that ever were held in this place. At half past 10 o'clock in the morning, public worship was commenced. Prayers were read by The Reverend D L Crowther, and a most impressive and practical sermon was preached by the Bishop from Acts XIII 1-3. There were present 469 persons, amongst whom were several European merchants, and nearly all the Bonny Chiefs.

After the sermon, the Ordination Service was performed by the Bishop, assisted by The Reverend James White, The Reverend W Morgan and the Reverend D C Crowther. The candidates were Reverend J Johnson, The Reverend Joseph During and myself. A more deeply interesting scene, it is scarcely possible to think of. It is unnecessary to describe the curious eagerness with which the natives sat or stood looking on while the ceremony was being performed. I trust however, they were much affected with the solemn proceedings. After ordination the Lord's Supper was administered, and all of us in the Mission partook of the same.

In the evening the Reverend J Johnson read prayers and the Reverend D L Crowther preached from Exodus XIV 15. After the second lesson, five male converts were admitted into the visible Church of Christ by the holy rite of Baptism. The Bishop baptised the first of them, I the next two and the Reverend D C Crowther the remaining two. These form the first fruits of this Mission. To God be all the praise and glory for the measure of success with which he has thus blessed our labours!

December 25th – Christmas Day 1872

Divine Service commenced at 11 o'clock. Mr. Crowther read the prayers, and, after the second lesson assisted me in administering the Sacrament of Baptism to four male converts. After the performance of the ceremony I addressed the congregation, which numbered no less than 400 souls, from Luke II 11. Amongst my hearers were many heathens whose feet, during the whole round of the year never crossed the threshold of the house of God but who however came today to join us in commemorating and meditating upon the birth of the World's Redeemer.

All were seriously attentive to my discourse, and many appeared deeply impressed with it. At the close of the service many walked over to our house to express to us the compliments of the joyful season, and lingered with pleasure on the premises in order to have a view of the animated diversions with which the boys passed the remaining part of the happy day.

It gives us very great pleasure to state that of the four candidates baptised today, that persecuted but resolute steward, spoken of the 23rd ultimo, was one. He passed through the ordeal with making a compromise of his faith and therefore proved himself worthy of admission into the visible Church of Christ. He received in addition to his native name, the Christian name of Daniel, to which he had a peculiar fancy and of which he himself had made a choice. My prayer for him and the others is, "that he who hath begun a good work in them may perform the same until the day of Jesus Christ."

December 31st

The last day in the year! The last Lord's day. How rapidly time speeds on its course! Surely "the time cometh when no man can work." And yet how little husbanded is this limited working-time of life's short day! How much is it mis-improved and misspent. It grieves me to think of the record of departed time, the mass of wasted years.

May the Lord enable me by his holy spirit to "redeem the time" which now lies before me, by availing myself more diligently than ever of every opportunity of preaching the word and winning souls of Christ.

January 3rd 1873

The Civil War by which, during the last three years this country has been unhappily torn and distracted, was fully brought to a termination today by means of arbitration. Mr. Consul Livingstone, Commodore Cornmerill and some native chiefs of New Calabar and Okrika were the arbitrators. The proceedings which were opened on New Year's Day resulted in a Treaty of Peace, which was made and signed today by Oko Jumbo and his party on the one side, and Juju and his party on the other side. It is to be hoped that both sides will faithfully fulfil the conditions and strictly adhere to the stipulations, therein involved, so that a long uninterrupted period of political tranquillity may be enjoyed, our missionary operations steadily carried on in safety and quietness and the native mind permitted to remain calm and composed to take under serious consideration the chains of our holy religion.

14*th* May 1873

The arrival of fetish gods of Toro-dig-bo gave me much pleasure. They were forwarded to me in a box and consisted of a heap of mere rubbish – a confused mass of bones, pieces of wood, clay, rags, dust etc. and yet have hitherto been the sacred objects of worship kept by a reasonable being! Oh how constantly ought we to put forth the prayer – "Pity blind idolaters who are kept in cruel bondage by the God of this world!"

May 22nd 1873

Ascension Day. Celebrated Divine Worship at 11 o'clock. Prayers having been read by Mr. Crowther, I preached from Luke XXIV 51-52. There were 100 of the natives present of whom 46 were adults and 54 children.

In the morning Mr. Crowther and myself called the chiefs to a meeting in town, and spoke with them on some secular matters. The first subject was introduced by Mr. Crowther who read a pamphlet containing the appeal for funds recently made by Bishop Crowther to the friends of missions in England. His Majesty the King was in attendance, and kindly explained to his chiefs in the vernacular what was read to them, and offered a short conversation on the subject amongst themselves. They expressed themselves much pleased with, and thankful for what the Bishop had done, requesting Mr. Crowther at the same time to acquaint his father, on their behalf, with their feelings on the subject. It then devolved upon me to call their attention to the Boarding School House now completed and laying vacant. As well as to the wretched and dangerous state of the road between the Mission Station and the Capital. A short discussion then ensued, after which they replied in reference to the first point that, owing to the absence in the plantation of some of the parents and guardians of the pupils, they felt obliged to postpone the consideration of the same till another occasion when those absent, should have returned to town, at which time they themselves will convene a meeting to reconsider the matter with regard to the road question, the reply was that it would receive their prompt and careful attention.

On Domestic Slavery and Punishment Illustrated in Journal of 14th September 1873

Lord's Day there was attendance at Divine Service of 163 of the natives in this morning, and 134 in the evening.

Of these, some were the identical persons who suffered last Sunday for coming to Church. The chief who inflicted an order to prevent the rest who also suffered, from coming, sent them into the woods to gather fuel. I received a shocking information this morning that the same chief caused one of his slaves to be strangled to death yesterday after first causing his two feet to be most brutally cut off with a sharp cutlass!! This horrid murder was perpetuated on no other ground than that the poor victim had run away into the interior, from whence he had just been recaptured. The chief said he did it as a public example to the rest of the slaves.

All these things amongst quite a cloud of other similar cruel deeds, serve clearly to illustrate not only that "The dark places of the earth are full of the habitations of cruelty" but also that the nefarious system of slavery in whatever form it appears, and by whatever name men may be pleased to call it – slavery foreign or domestic – is beyond a doubt a curse to Africa and to humanity.

NB This being 1873! 40 years after emancipation of slavery in the British Empire.

2nd November 1873

The Lord's Day. Conducted Divine Worship at the usual hours. The evening service was of some special interest. There were in attendance the native troops who were on the eve of embarking on board the mail steamer for <u>Cape Coast Castle</u> to join <u>The Ashanti Expedition</u>.

King George Pepple and his two brothers Princes Henry and Charles, the latter of whom being the officer in command of the troops, were also present. It was a novel sight at this place and an interesting occasion. Preached on these words of the Psalmist, "Some trust in chariots, and some in horses; but we will remember the name of our God" Psalms 20 verse 7.

Proceeding as they expected very shortly to do to scenes of bloodshed and the theatre of war, I embraced the opportunity of pointing out to these soldiers how foolish and vain it was for any people to trust upon their arms and their warlike equipment, and all other earthly resources, on the one hand, and of recommending to them on the other the Name of the Lord as being a "Strong Tower" and the only source of all protection, safety and victory. In conclusion, I urged them solemnly to adopt the Psalmist's resolution as expressed in the text and to hold it as their motto during the perilous campaign. Nearly 300 souls were present and all seemed deeply solemnized and impressed by the sermon.

Letter from Christopher Fyfe to the author

London

2nd March 2006

Dear Victor

Many thanks for sending me the report of Rev. Frederick Smart's sermon to the native troops on their way to the Ashanti Expedition – a most appropriate sermon with a well chosen text for soldiers off to war. It will make a splendid contribution to your work. My congratulations to Ruth for locating the CMS microfilms.

It interests me for another quite different reason. King George Pepple was ruler of Opobo, one of the trading states of the Niger Delta where, for over 300 years, a flourishing export trade had been carried on, first in slaves, then in palm-oil. Just before this time he had been deposed by JaJa, a powerful trader, and had gone into exile with his followers, presumably to Lagos, which was by this time under British rule, and offered his services to the government.

The Ashanti Expedition was under the command of Sir Garnet Wolseley who was anxious to make himself appear as a great military commander and saw to it that his very minor campaign was given the utmost publicity – indeed it was the first British military campaign to be given full press coverage. Stanley, the famous explorer, was one of the journalists reporting it and some of the officers subsequently published books about it, glorifying a war in which only one small battle was fought, the Ashanti army retreated inland, Wolseley's force moved rapidly inland, burnt Kumasi, the Ashanti capital, and returned equally rapidly home where five officers were awarded Victoria Crosses! Wolseley insisted on bringing white troops so these native troops never saw any action.

I know all this in detail from the research I did for my biography of Africanus Horton who took part in the campaign as a medical officer – and to his indignation received no recognition.

With best wishes to you both

Christopher

Christmas Day 1873

600 attended service, St Stephen's Bonny

Christmas Day. Had a finishing touch part to the church decoration with the flowers at dawn. Before service, bell was rung, crowds of natives began to flow in from every quarter and when I entered to commence Divine Worship at 11 o'clock, I found to my great surprise and joy that an immense congregation, consisting men, women and children, had thronged the building to the very door, while many were trooping up and hurrying along on the road to enter in and swell the numbers. Some coming as worshippers and others as curious sightseers. It is perhaps needless for me to confess that with such a motley mass of semi-civilized and heathen people I found it difficult, if not impossible, to ensure order and decorum at the outset, but by dint of perseverance, I succeeded to put down all vulgar jostling and noise, and to arrange those within in order, as best as lay in my power.

This being done, I commenced Divine Worship but I had only announced the hymn – "Hark the Herald Angel sings" – when a heathen man observing his wife among the number of those set apart to be baptised rose up in the midst of the assembly and began to speak in a rather boisterous tone, threatening the poor woman with severe punishment if she received baptism, against his will, on the one hand, and appealing to the congregation for their aid by way of requesting me, on his behalf, not to baptise her on the other.

In vain did I endeavour to quiet the disturbing man. In vain did some of his friends endeavour to persuade him not to oppose God's work in his own house. This rage grew from bad to worse, the more he was spoken to in a reasonable way – a *mighty contrast to his wife who sat quietly looking on with composure and meekness depicted on her very countenance and as resolved to receive baptism as her husband was to thwart it. Finding, however, that his excitement only afforded merriment to those who came merely as spectators, and displeasure to those who came as devout worshippers. That his wife was firm in her resolution, and that I was nothing – but quite prepared to perform a duty which I owed to my Divine Master and to the candidate.*

He rushed out and ran to town with a view of laying his complaint before the chiefs. Silence being once more restored, service was proceeded with. As I was reading the Second lesson a messenger came up and informed me that orders have been dispatched by the chief to inform me that I should not baptise that woman. I sent a reply to say that the Lord had commanded me to baptise all who were believers in him and were willing to receive baptism and that I was bound to obey God rather than man. Soon after the second lesson, therefore, I forthwith entered upon the baptismal office. The woman in question was accordingly baptised, in company with eight candidates. She was named Christina Obonne; she rejoiced greatly that she was not seized away by force, by her husband, and I was myself thankful for this. No further interruption was caused the remaining part of the days' proceedings.

Luke 2.15 formed the basis of my discourse on this joyous occasion. Great power of utterance and boldness of spirit were given me to make known to my hearers the great mystery of godliness on the one hand, and to vindicate in an unforgivable manner on the other the principle upon which I went to administering the sacrament of baptism to those who were on the occasion added to the Lord. Breathless was the silence, marked the occasion, and I believe, deep was the impression, pervading the vast assembly. It is estimated that the number of my audience cannot fall short of six hundred!

At the close of the service the newly baptised were greeted by the native converts with great joy; and we may well believe that there was joy also in the presence of the angels of God over these souls newly won to Christ. May these converts be enabled by the influence of Divine Spirit, to adorn the doctrine of God, their Saviour in all things and so to live and walk worthy of the vocation wherewith they are called. That their friends and neighbours and countrymen may "take knowledge of them that they have been with Jesus".

He ended his journal for this date with these words:-

May 15th 1876 – Announcing the death of his wife.

I must close this report by announcing with emotions of the profoundest grief that on Sunday 27th February, my dear partner in life was removed by death to her heavenly home. She has left me to grapple alone with the toils and trials of a Missionary life, and left to my care, beside a little boy, not three years old, a tender baby girl who was born only on the 9th January last! But thanks be to God, I am able most confidently to record that her end was most peaceful, most happy and most triumphant. It is impossible for me with so limited a space to give "any" detailed account of her last illness and death.

I shall therefore content myself with stating briefly that a few days before to her most deeply lamented removal, she said, "I have found Christ to be my Saviour, my mediator and my redeemer." On being asked by me concerning her hope, she replied, "Christ is my hope! He only!"

On another occasion she said, "Living or dying, I am safe in the arms of Jesus". She often sang these beautiful lines "Heaven is my fatherland, Heaven is my home."

Last of all she was heard to exclaim, "Thank God, I have overcome at last." As well as to pray, "Come Lord Jesus, come quickly, come and receive my spirit." Her mortal remains now lies in the soil of this place.

This is indeed a painful and mysterious stroke of God's providence, and I can find no words to fully express how keenly I feel the afflictive blow, but amidst my moans and tears, I desire to echo forth the words "Thy will be done".

6

Letters

Letter 1

Reverend Frederick Smart CAI/027/66: Mr. Smart to Reverend H J Alcock.

His letter of August 16th 1869 to his friend Reverend H J Alcock mentioned the question of his speculation for a future partner. His sister was on the look out in Sierra Leone for some one suitable.

Letter 2

With reference to Frederick's resignation letter (CAI/023) Letter 77 Taylor noted the difference between the Saros (Creoles from Sierra Leone returning back to Nigeria) and those returning to Yorubaland and to the Niger area [19]. This was reflected in the conditions of service. The Yoruba Saros tended to settle down in Yorubaland whereas those in the Niger Mission saw themselves as expatriates and expected financial support for the mission for passages for themselves and their families to and from Freetown.

Reverend Smart's letter reflected a huge disappointment and feeling of let down and uncaring support by the Mission Headquarters and Personnel in London and by Bishop Crowther (that must have been a really cruel blow). Hence his letter of resignation from the Niger Mission.

Letter 3

Letter from Frederick Smart to Reverend Wright, Salisbury Square, London. Ref CAI/073/84A

This letter, written from his home at Regent in 1878, conveys the feeling of despair and regret over his decision of resigning from the Niger Mission nearly two years earlier. He was prepared to make a short visit to Headquarters in London to plead his case for atonement.

After serving in the Mission since 1868 when he was stationed at Bonny, Nigeria, he resigned in 1876. He felt himself forced to take this extreme step because of his unhappiness with certain rules and regulations of the Church Missionary Society which could be described as discriminating against African Priests compared with the experience of white missionaries.

(Letter 1: Mr. Smart to Reverend H J Alcock)

Mission Houses
Bonny

August 16th 1869

Rev. and very dear Sir,

Your truly kind and friendly letter dated July 19th duly came to hand and was read and reread with unusual delight and gratitude.

I particularly remark the warm interest you take in me and I shall ever consider it a treat to hear from you as often as opportunity offers.

I am much rejoiced to hear that you are in hopes of taking a trip down these parts in October coming DV. I shall indeed constitute one of my most happy days to see you here in person on that occasion, I pray therefore that no unforeseen occurrences should turn up to frustrate your plans for October.

With regard to the commentary. I beg to say that there is none which I had for myself that which I had when in the college you requested me to learn for the use of the students, promising to write home for some copies, one of which you would send down for me, since then I have been making use of a copy which I was fortunate enough to meet here in the Mission.

I shall therefore be very much obliged if you shall be pleased to bring with you what you intend giving me. I am really thankful that in distributing the books that were at your disposal, you did not forget to reserve some for me.

Respecting the important subject of marriage I can assure you that it has already begun to occupy my serious consideration.

I have already sent home several letters and my sister is already at work considering a young person who has been recommended. I am consequently waiting to see how the wind blows in that direction before I make any decisive move.

It seems so difficult in these days to decide at once about any particular girl!

Matters being in this position at present, I would therefore beg to express my regret that I could not possibly give you any decided reply concerning the young ladies whom you are kind enough to recommend.

I nevertheless do safely hope that you would unite with me in commending the whole affair to the superintending direction and guidance of our kind and Almighty Father who taketh <u>special</u> interest in the <u>temporal</u> no less than the eternal concerns of his erring and short-sighted children.

I really mourn and grieve after the scandalous fall of poor Cates. It was a sad affair.

This is surely a great warning to us to keep closer and closer to Jesus, whose grace is sufficient for us whose strength shall be made perfect in our weakness. May God have mercy on Cates, may his wreck prove our beacon!

I am glad to state that we are hard at work here I am trying hard not to let a single day pass without sowing some seeds for Christ. I really delight in the missionary work.

Though we cannot just now boast of any decided convert yet. I have every reason to believe that the leaven of gospel truth is really and powerfully at work.

Several Natives have been convinced of the vanity and foolishness of idolatry and superstition and have abandoned them and are attending the House of God every Lord's day. They only want a little more decision to come forward despite the persecuting rage and scoffs of their country people, whom, like Nicodemus in the days of our Lord, they greatly dread.

May God soon bestow upon them true faith and resolution. The people are now taken up with celebrating a feast of their gods and there is no end of eating and drinking and dancing and merry making.

Nor do they do these things during the day only, but they pass all the night in such practices, even this <u>very</u> moment as my pen is on this paper I hear some of the drums in the neighbourhood. The feast lasts eight days and is important to them as any of the three great feasts was to the Jews. It has some connection with the in gathering of the new corn and new yam. It is called in the native dialect – "A-la-le".

I must now come to a close. Rev. Crowther has gone up the river.

Remember me to all kind Christian friends, with hopes to see you here, in short, I beg to remain Rev. and very dear Sir with sentiments of gratitude and affection,

Yours respectfully

F W Smart

(Letter 2: Mr. Smart to Rev. Crowther)

Freetown[20]
Sierra Leone

October 9th 1876

Right Rev. and dear Sir,

Yours bearing date 15th July duly came to hand and received an attentive perusal from me.

Presuming that by this time you are on your homeward voyage to the coast from your usual annual visitation tour up the river Niger, I hasten to address you the following lines in reply.

Please do accept my sincere apology for my omitting to state in my last the reasons which have decided me to dissolve all connection with the Niger Mission. The omission arose not from the want of good and weighty reasons on my part but from an earnest desire to avoid stating anything that might give rise to any needless offence on the part of one whom I most deeply revere.

But since neither yourself nor the Parent Committee of the Church Missionary Society can feel satisfied with the course I have found it necessary to adopt, without my stating them I feel bound in duty to you and the Society as well as in justice to myself, and to all concerned to submit to you the reasons which have induced me to forego my further continuance and labours in that Mission.

Apart from those of a more personal or private character I have to submit the following two reasons:-

1) The arrangements made for the Missionaries ordained and unordained as regards their passage on board the Mail Steamers from Sierra Leone to the Niger and vice versa are such as I have found it totally impossible to adhere to. Although our stipends or salaries are far below what our brethren at home are receiving from the Society, and are quite inadequate! So the ordinary demands upon our purses in such localities on the banks of the Niger and the Delta as we have to labour in, where provisions and other necessary articles are scarce and high in price – yet Missionaries visiting home after a number of years of active service in the field or sending their wives and children, separately or together, who may be in a state of ill health, or, under some pressing necessity to visit home, are required to pay out of the same, a part of the passage money, homewards and outwards for themselves and wives, and the whole of the passage money for the members of their families (who may have increased in numbers during their stay in the field) or are left to the necessity of taking, at the Mission's charges a forsaken passage for themselves and wives (though in case their wives are sent home alone, their passage is required to be paid by their husbands) while the members of their families are paid for by themselves.

It cannot be denied for it is indisputably patent to all, that the forecabin passage in such Mail Steamers as are running along our coast, with hardly any exception, is most unsuitable to the sacredness and noble cause we seek to advance, most uncomparable to the missionaries themselves and most unsafe to their luggage and baggage.

You are aware that when in 1873, I found it highly necessary to send my late dear partner from Bonny to Sierra Leone I had to pay her passage myself on her leaving and returning to the Mission. Also that in April last after her removal by death, which I most deeply deplore under most painful circumstances when you kindly gave me permission to bring the poor tender babe, whom she left behind, together with my little boy, to Sierra Leone not withstanding a most urgent request on my part to the contrary, I had to be left under the necessity of paying part of my own passage home, besides paying wholly for one of the children, for the babes nurse and for a relative of my late wife's who came to assist me in the care of the children. These heavy expenses I can assure you, have now placed me in most embarrassing circumstances. And as the same paying process will have to be gone through over and over again and the evil here complained of be thus aggravated, as it has been originated, by the same I have in consequence felt myself compelled to dissolve my connection with the Niger Mission.

2 The regulations made for the wives of the Niger Missionaries are so unusual and unsatisfactory that I cannot conscientiously continue in that Mission without acting, on principle, in opposition to them.

I refer to the regulations which require all the educated wives of all the Missionaries ordained or unordained to be reckoned as "female teachers" of the Society.

Although there can be no reasonable doubt or question that the wives of all Missionaries are expected to give a hearty and willing co-operation to their husbands in their work yet if I understand the Society's Rules and Regulations. As well as the statistics in reference to the actual number of their "female teachers" in all their other Missions aright it seems to me perfectly evident that a clear and marked distinction is made between the wives of the Missionaries and female teachers.

When you first proposed this scheme to us I felt it my duty candidly and respectfully to express my mind to you on the subject, but I am now perfectly convinced by your remarks on the eve of my leaving Bonny for Sierra Leone in April last that the regulations in question would be rigidly enforced by you. Now, therefore, that my wife is no more and I am once more at home I feel that it is in my wisdom and safety to withdraw myself, in time and in peace from that Mission.

For I could not endure the penalty to be imposed in case the regulations be not attended to by anyone that is a curtailment of the Missionary salary stipend, already inadequate, and also a deprivation of all assistance and support on the part of the Mission to his widow, in case he should be removed by death; necessary labours out of the schoolroom, whether on Sundays or weekdays among the heathen or Christian portion of the female population.

The above, Sir, are the two main causes on public grounds which have operated on my mind to bring about the result which I communicated to you in my last and sincerely hope that nothing I have said will give any personal offence.

I am sure you will deem it far better, as alas I do, that I should adopt the course to which I have at last had recourse, than unwillingly continue in the Mission, thinking contrary to your expressed and firm opinion and acting in opposition to your high and venerable authority.

May I therefore be allowed humbly and respectfully to crave at your hands the favour of a testimonial or letter recommendatory, which I may present to the Bishop of Sierra Leone so as to have a door of influences opened to me in this portion of the Lord's vineyard.

Begging your pardon for encroaching so much upon your valuable time by this lengthy letter and commending myself to your forbearance and sympathy.

I have the honour to remain
Right Rev. and dear Sir
Your obedient humble Servant
F W Smart

The Right Rev. S A Crowther DD
Bishop of the Niger Territory

(Letter 3: Mr. Smart to Rev. Wright, London)

Liverpool Street[21]
Regent
Sierra Leone
West Africa

March 5th 1878

Rev. Wright
   Salisbury Square
     Islington
       London

Rev. and Dear Sir,

    I crave the liberty of addressing you the following lines on a subject of the deepest importance to myself and I venture to hope that they will meet with a favourable reception.

    Permit me to state for your information that it is now almost two years since my retirement from the Niger Mission. And I can assure you that words fail me to describe how earnest has been my desire during that period to be received as an Agent in connection with the Society's work in Sierra Leone, or that of the Native Church.

    But I have found, with profound regret that certain difficulties of a serious character have arisen, preventing a door being opened to me in this portion of the Lord's vineyard. The Right Reverend Bishop Crowther who was justly offended at the manner I withdrew from the Mission of which he is the head, has not been pleased to overlook or pardon my misconduct notwithstanding that I have done everything in my power to make peace with him. Under these difficult and anxious circumstances therefore I can see no other course open to me to adopt then asking the favour of a permission from the Parent Committee to take a short visit to England with a view to lay open to them in person what cannot be fully done in writing, the real state of my feelings.

Should my request be kindly entertained I would deem it no burden to undertake the expense of the visit, whatever it may cost me.

The privilege of labouring in the Service of that noble and evangelical Society of which you are one of the leading Secretaries and to which I owe a lasting debt of gratitude as well as of devolving my feeble efforts by way of ministerial usefulness to the advancement of the Redeemers cause and for the salvation of the perishing souls is one which, I beg leave to confess, I really cannot bring my mind to be willing to forego No other employment however lucrative can give me satisfaction.

I most humbly and most earnestly pray therefore that you may be graciously pleased to take a compassionate and benevolent view of my case and to exercise, on my behalf that fatherly sympathy for which the most urgent necessity of my present situation has strongly induced me to hope.

Anxiously awaiting a reply to my appeal.

I have the honour to remain
Rev. and dear Sir
Your obedient humble servant

F W Smart

Despite genuine attempts to rejoin the Niger Mission, which were unsuccessful, Rev. Smart reluctantly abandoned his idea. His next big move was to open a Boys' High School in Pademba Road, Freetown, in 1879 but it faded away after a few years and he was later appointed to the government school at Accra.[22]

The following was advertised in the The West African Reporter, February 10th 1883.

SMART'S HIGH SCHOOL

The Principal and Proprietor of the above mentioned private educational establishment continues to receive boys of all ages. (boarders as well as day scholars) for a thorough tuition, Classics, Mathematics, Logic, Vocal Music, Book-Keeping, English Composition and every branch of a high class English Education, carefully taught.

General arrangements made for giving private lessons, also young men desirous of qualifying themselves for the Civil, Mercantile or any other service. Terms very moderate, prospectus on application. Address:-
The Rev. F W Smart, 1 Pademba Road, Freetown.

Following the closure of his school he proceeded to Accra (then the Gold Coast), Ghana, with his second wife Justina (née Johnson), where he taught in the Government School. They settled in Accra. Unfortunately, Reverend Smart lost his wife in 1887. Her death was published in The Weekly News dated February 5th 1887. It read:

> The death at Accra in the Gold Coast Colony, of Mrs. Justina Smart has been announced. Mrs. Smart was the daughter of Pilot Johnson of Freetown and married some years ago to the Rev. F W Smart. We sympathise with the deceased relative.

Just over a year following Mrs. Smart's death, Rev. F W Smart passed away. His death was announced in the Weekly News dated April 28th 1888.

> It was on the 18th instant that the death of the Rev. F W Smart, Master of the Colonial Government School at Accra, was reported, it concluded. 'We express out sympathy with the friends and relatives of the deceased, and say to each of our readers "Live mindful of death".'

The years following his resignation and attempt to be readmitted to the Niger Mission without success, must have been sad and pitiful for Reverend Frederick Smart.

Disappointing for him also, was the closure of his school after only a few years. However, I am convinced his life took a turn for the better when he was appointed a teacher to the Government School in Accra, it is possible that his salary would have been higher than what he was paid when he served as a Missionary with the Niger Mission. Assuming that he had a higher salary, his standard of life no doubt must have been more comfortable. It is difficult to think whether he got over his rejection of not being readmitted again to the Niger Mission.

Frederick was survived by his son and daughter of his first wife, who died when William and Mary were quite young, Mary only a few months old.

They were raised by family members in Regent, where they went to primary school, after which William moved to the Cathedral School, then to the Grammar School, which he entered in 1888, his registration number being 1357. Mary, according to family traditions, would have eventually gone to the Annie Walsh Memorial School. After completing her secondary education, she proceeded to England to train as a teacher, but unfortunately she died before completing her studies.

William trained to become a druggist and later moved to the Gambia (Banjul) where he settled and raised his children Dan and Onike. He had married Regina Williams from a well known and respected Freetown family.

William would, from time to time, visit his homeland. In an advert on the Sierra Leone Weekly News, 30th August 1919, would be found this announcement:

> Mr. William Sylvanus Smart (druggist of Bathurst, Gambia), who had been spending his holiday for a few months in Freetown, on a visit to his uncle Doctor Randle and was guest of Mr. O J Benjamin of East Street, left by the Onitsha of the 18th inst on his return to Bathurst.

William must have been highly successful in his professional work in the Gambia because he was eventually appointed as a Justice of the Peace. Quite an important acknowledgement in recognition of valuable work done within the community. Three years after his visit to Freetown the following was found under General News in The Sierra Leone Weekly News:

> **DEATH OF MR. SMART**
>
> It is with deep regret that we have to record the death of Mr. William Sylvanus Smart JP, who passed away on Sunday afternoon 4th inst at the residence of Mr. O J Benjamin in East Street .... It appears Mr. Smart took ill suddenly just a few days before his death ..... His remains were removed to Regent, his birth place, interred in the cemetery, deeply regretted Mr. Smart left his widow and children at Bathurst. We express our sympathy to his widow and children and other relatives.[23]

His family remained in the Gambia where his son would train to become a druggist like his father. After some years Mrs. Smart and daughter Onike returned and settled in Freetown at No 22, Charlotte Street.

Dan, did very well in his profession, was well respected in Bathurst, married and had the following children, Eallaleen, Reginald, Daniel, Ivor and Zein.

Daniel Weeks Smart
Grandson of Frederick Weeks Smart

Onike, his sister, married dentist John. Unfortunately she lost her husband in a drowning incident early in their marriage. There were no children.

Aunty Oni would eventually play a major role in various women's organisations representing Sierra Leone in international women's conferences all over the world. In the 60s she became the Mayoress of Freetown, with Mrs. Constance Cummings-John (her sister-in-law), the Mayor. She died suddenly in 1978.

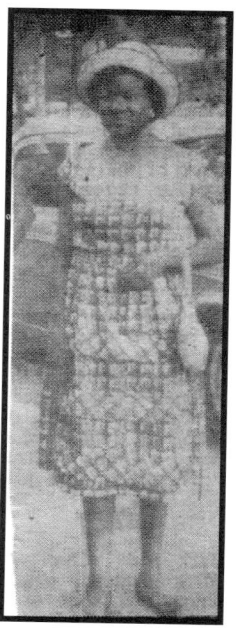

Mrs. Onike John née Smart,
Grand-daughter of
Frederick Weeks-Smart

7

Francis John Smart 1841 – 1894

My great grandfather, Francis, who like his twin brother had an excellent education was a pupil at the grammar school, which he entered on First July 1861. His enrolment number being 388.

The Old Grammar School, Regent Square, Freetown.

It is interesting to note that his twin brother Frederick had entered the grammar school a year earlier. I discovered that Francis suffered with deafness and it is possible that it could have held him back a year. Unlike his brother who was in the ministry and then a missionary to Bonny, Francis became interested in teaching. Teaching as a profession appealed to many, both ordained and secular among the Krio elite. It was possible for some to have a successful and satisfactory career in the eyes of British authorities.

Francis enjoyed a successful career in teaching. The Blue Books of 1870 and subsequent years up to 1890, listed him in charge of the Government school at Cassa, Factory Island, Isle de Los. In 1894, the school was closed, and Francis was retired on a pension on medical grounds. In his letter, Acting Governor Crooks, declared that Mr. Marke, the School Inspector, felt himself able to give a certificate on 23rd January 1894 that Mr. F J Smart had "discharged his duties with diligence and fidelity".[24]

In a letter from Crooks Administrator to the Right Honourable The Marquis of Ripon KG dated 20th February 1894, a paragraph in that letter stated:

> 'In his despatch W42 of 30th ultimo Sir F Fleming forwarded for your Lordships, consideration the pension papers in the case of Mr. F J Smart who for twenty three years had been the Government school master at Isles de Los, and who has been pronounced unfit for further service by the medical officers due to ill health.'[25]

The nature of his illness was not specified. However, with my knowledge of family medical history and after further discussion with the late Dr. Robert Wellesley-Cole, grandson of Francis Smart, we can say that he probably had a complication, relating to diabetes and with a history of deafness this would have resulted in a rapid deterioration in his health. Hence his retirement at the age of 53 years. On a Board of Education Document 1894 the following was noted.

Office	Name	Date of Appointment	By whom selected and whether appointment under an instrument	Annual Salary
Education Department	M J Marke	4th Jan 1893	Secretary of State	£250
Inspector of Schools	Jacob W Lewis	4th Jan 1893	Governor	£20
Clerk to Board of Education				
Government School Isles de Los Master	F J Smart	2nd August 1870	Governor	£36

26

£36 in Sierra Leone was equivalent to £3,500 in 1890. Information from Lloyds Bank official in Victorian village at the Ironbridge Gorge, Shropshire. The Lloyds Bank official's estimate that £36 in 1870 would be £3,500 today seems to me perfectly acceptable. But we must remember that £36 was Francis's **annual** salary, giving him today £291 per month, £67 per week with a family of seven children to support, well below any poverty line. Admittedly, life on the Isle de Los was cheap, but he will have had to wear a suit and boots, and you may be sure that the people were always coming to him for one thing or another. My impression is that the only other government official on the islands was sub-collector of customs, so he no doubt functioned as an unofficial magistrate. Well, I hope it was a satisfying and enjoyable life for a man whose deafness may have limited his ambitions.

As for the three salaries quoted above, the differentials between his salary and theirs was even greater than appears. Marke received another £160 as Inspector of Schools in the Gambia. Lewis was the Governor's Clerk, with £260 salary; this £20 must have been some added little perquisite. Head Clerks in government offices received £75 – and when extra clerks had to be taken on they were paid £36 per **month**.

In a further despatch the following is noted regarding F J Smart:

Name of Pensioner	*Amount of Pension sterling*	*Authority under which the pension was granted.*
Francis John Smart	*£ s d* *16.11.2 ½*	*Secretary of State Despatch No 33 of 2First February, 1894*
		Date from which the pension has been paid First February 1894.[27]

Incidentally, until the Church of England was disestablished in Sierra Leone in 1896, the government paid a salary of £200 to a Colonial Chaplain for sitting comfortably at home in Freetown and taking the services in the Cathedral – twice what the CMS paid their missionaries and pastors.

Francis thus retired and settled in his village of Regent. There is no account of his physical health. Unfortunately, he only survived for another four months since he retired in February. He died in June 1894 and was buried, aged 53 years, in the village cemetery.

8

Francis was survived by his wife Mary (née Aboko-Cole) and seven children.

Name	Details	School	Register Number	Year Entered
John	Grandfather's eldest brother; died 1901 in South Africa where he was a Missionary.	Grammar School	1283	1886
Frederick	Worked at Customs Department. Premature retirement, became ill.			
Francis	Author's Grandfather, prolific writer, farmer and builder.	Grammar School	1458	1891
Benjamin	Grandfather's younger brother. Worked initially as a Missionary in the Limba Country later progressed to The Treasury in Nigeria.	Grammar School	1634	1894

Name	Details	School	Register Number	Year Entered
Benjamin (cont'd)	Proceeded to England. Qualified as a Doctor in 1925.	Grammar School	1634	1894
Elizabeth Beatrice	Married to Wilfred Wellesley-Cole. Water Engineer, Freetown.	Annie Walsh Memorial School		
Daniel	Youngest brother of Grandfather. Most of his life in Conakry, Guinea, teaching French.	Grammar School	2052	1904
Mary	Married Mr. Uriah Taylor	Annie Walsh Memorial School		

Frederick Okrafor-Smart. Born about 1872, his early schooling took place at Regent then he went to the Grammar School. Oral history says that he was quite brilliant and after leaving school went on to work at The Customs Department as a Civil Servant. He later became seriously ill and could not work again until his death in the early 1940s. Was not married and no children.

Okrafo-Smart Family:
Over a Century in the Lives of a Liberated African Family

103

A PHOTOGRAPH TAKEN IN 1919

Standing left to right:
Dr. Robert Wellesley-Cole, Mr. Wilfred Sidney Wellesley-Cole, Arthur brother of Robert
Granny Florence Cole (Wilfred's mother), Elizabeth née Okrafor-Smart, Mary Okrafor-Smart (wife of Francis – Master of Government School Isle de Los) holding Eric younger brother of Robert.
Sitting on ground; Phoebe and Irene sisters of Robert, Arthur and Eric.

John Okrafor-Smart, the eldest son of my great grandfather Francis and his wife Mary, was born in 1870 at Regent. He started school at Regent then continued at Isle de Los where his father was the master in charge of the Government school. He later moved to the Grammar School to complete his secondary education, his admission number was 1283 on the register. As with the family history he was trained for the Ministry. He later left Sierra Leone and went as a Missionary to South Africa, where he died in 1901.

His sister, Mrs. Elizabeth Wellesley-Cole, presented a silver plate to St Charles Church, Regent, in his memory. On the inside of the silver plate is written "Gift of Mrs. Eliza B Cole in memory of her late brother John W Smart who died in 1901 in South Africa".

He was 31 years of age. It is likely he went as a Chaplain to the African non-combatant labour force during this period of the Boer War.

Benjamin Okrafor-Smart was the fourth child of great grandfather Francis. As with other male members of the family, after early education at Regent he entered the Grammar School in 1894, his registration number being 1634.

Dr. Benjamin Okrafor –Smart
MB., BS., MA. (1925)

After the Grammar School he went to Fourah Bay College on a CMS scholarship, from here he graduated with a BA in theology. He then worked as a Missionary and served in the then Protectorate for five years, before going to Nigeria where he worked in the Treasury Department, Lagos. During this time he saved diligently in order to pursue his life's ambition which was to qualify as a Doctor. At the age of 40 he proceeded to England and entered medical school at Newcastle. He subsequently qualified as a Doctor in 1925. Here is a publication in the Sierra Leone Weekly News dated April 18th 1925 to announce his successes.

> 'Dr. Okrafor-Smart, MA, MB, BS (Durham). We are pleased to learn that Mr. Alfred Benjamin Weeks Okrafor-Smart has graduated in the School of Medicine and Surgery at the University of Durham.
>
> 'Dr. Smart was educated at the Grammar School and at Fourah Bay College where he graduated BA in Arts and Theology. On leaving the college he laboured as a CMS missionary in the Limba and Yalinka Countries in Northern Sierra Leone until withdrawal of the CMS from the Protectorate. In 1908 when he joined the Nigerian Civil Service where he rose to the rank of First Class Officer in the Treasury Department. He resigned the Civil Service in 1918 and proceeded to England to pursue the study of Medicine. We wish him every success in the practice of his profession.
>
> 'Dr. Okrafor-Smart is brother of Mr. F W Okrafor-Smart, builder and agriculturist and of Mrs. W S Wellesley-Cole.'

In the 30th May 1925 Sierra Leone Weekly News is an advert to welcome Dr. Okrafor-Smart on his arrival in Freetown;

> 'We are pleased to welcome to Sierra Leone a new medico in the person of Dr. A B Okrafor-Smart MA, MB, BS, who arrived from England through Holland and Antwerp by the steamship Alberto, on Wednesday 27th inst.
>
> 'Dr. Okrafor-Smart resided for 10 years in Nigeria to which place he is proceeding. He has broken his passage here to spend sometime with his relatives and friends both in Freetown and at the village of Regent. We had the pleasure of shaking hands with him and wished him every success in his practice in Nigeria. He will remain in Freetown for about a month.'

In Lagos he set up a flourishing practice at his home No 5 Dawoda Lane, Ebute Meta, Lagos, Nigeria.

He maintained his interest in the mission field and in the mid 1930s he underwent theological retraining and was eventually ordained in the Anglican Church and served as a pastor of All Saints Church, Yaba, Lagos. During this period, between 1930 and 1940, he was able to trace his ancestors. Oral history gives us the account that he visited Orlu Division in Imo State, Eastern Nigeria, and eventually founded a church at Itu-Isu near Alo-Chukuru. It was through his involvement with the church at this period that he was able to trace his ancestors, the original Okoroafor family.

He later brought some of his erstwhile relatives with him back to Lagos to stay on his land.

Dr. Benjamin married a Nigerian by the name of Kahinde. They were blessed with two daughters, Ajoke and Sarah.

Apart from his practice as a Doctor and later Priest in the Anglican Church "Uncle Benji" as he was called, participated in medical debates, lectures, etc. During the Fourth Session at Lagos of the National Congress of British West Africa, he presented a paper on "The Drink Traffic in West Africa". This was advertised as follows in the Sierra Leone Weekly News of 18th January 1930:

> TODAY CONGRESS SESSION
> FRIDAY 3RD JANUARY 9 AM 1930
>
> (1) The Drink Traffic in West Africa by Dr. A B W Okrafor-Smart MA., MB., BS., etc. etc.
> (2) The Position and Education of Womenhood-in-West-Africa and Constitutional Reforms by Dr. C C Adeniyi-Jones MA., MB., CHB., etc. etc.

Daniel Okrafor-Smart was the sixth child of great grandfather Francis, Master-in-Charge of Government School, Isle de Los.

As with his elder brothers, he started his education at Regent, and eventually to the Grammar School, registration number being 2052, and later proceeded to Fourah Bay College which he entered in 1907.

After graduation, he spent most of his teaching life in Dakar, Guinea. Not much is known of his own family life other than he had a son called Anthony. A list of my family – Smarts who went to Fourah Bay College before 1930 – could be found in a publication by T J Thompson; *The Jubilee and Centenary Volume of Fourah Bay College,* Sierra Leone (Freetown 1930). Listed in an appendix, the students from 1827 – 1929. These Smarts are listed.

>Frederick Smart (1864)
>Alfred Benjamin Weeks Smart (1900)
>Christian Jackson Adjou Smart (1907)
>Daniel Augustus Smart (1907)

The youngest of the seven children of great grandfather Francis was **Mary**. She married Mr. Uriah Taylor. He worked with the Cable and Wireless Department and spent most of his working life in the Congo. After her husband's retirement she stayed at Regent where she lived until her death aged 96 years. One of her children was Mrs. Emma Johnson. It was Aunt Emma (as we called her) who told me about the pioneering work of great grandfather Francis and his twin brother Frederick. The information got me interested and after preliminary research, I decided to write the history of my family.

Francis Okrafo-Smart 1874 – 1930. An intellectual, an entrepreneur, a builder, a writer, immense talents. His life will be covered in more detail later.

9

Elizabeth Beatrice Okrafo-Smart, later Mrs. Wellesley-Cole. Elizabeth started her early education at the school in Regent, and then proceeded to the Annie Walsh Memorial School, the premier girls school founded in 1849, four years after the grammar school, both of them ran by the Anglican missionaries.

Later Elizabeth became friendly with Wilfred Sydney Wellesley-Cole, who was very friendly with her brothers Francis and Benjamin who were all pupils at the grammar school. As a result the friendship developed and they got married eventually. Wilfred was very successful as a Water Engineer, and eventually became the Superintendent of the water department. He thus became the only black head of a public department, not only in Sierra Leone but in all colonial Africa.[28]

They were blessed with the following children:-

Robert Benjamin Ageh Wellesley-Cole (see document reproduced on page 117)	Surgeon
Arthur Blandford Ageh Wellesley-Cole	Barrister and Judge
Wilfred Ageh Wellesley-Cole	Died aged 2
Phoebe Winifred Elizabeth Wellesley-Cole (Mrs. Percy Jones)	Artist and Bishop's wife

Irene Beatrice Wellesley-Cole (Mrs. Sam Ighodaro) _{See document reproduced on page 122}	Medical Practitioner
Eric Soloman Ageh Wellesley-Cole	Engineer
Mabel Taiwo Wellesley-Cole (Mrs. Chariff)	Nursing Sister

Okrafo-Smart Family: Over a Century in the Lives of a Liberated African Family 113

Family Photograph on the occasion of Robert Wellesley-Cole leaving Freetown to study medicine 1928

Our family, mother's section. Sitting Francis Smart, father, mother, Benjamin Smart (Uncle Benji). Dan Smart. Standing: From left Sarah Smart, Arthur, Phoebe, me, Ajoke Smart, Idowu Smart, Frances Taylor, Irene. Right back: William Bultman, Balogun Smart. On the ground Eric (Morlai), Mabel, Orah Smart.

Robert Wellesley-Cole, perhaps the most brilliant of his generation. Born in 1907, he arrived in England in 1928, aged 21, with two British degrees. BA Durham Affiliate (Mathematics and Classics) and BA London External (Philosophy). At Newcastle on Tyne he qualified in Medicine in 1934, with first class honours in every examination, and won eighteen class and professional prizes and scholarships, plus one in philosophy.

Dr. Robert Wellesley - Cole

M.B., BS., MA., MD.,

F.R.C.S. Edin. (1944)

He became the first African to be elected a Fellow by examination, of the Royal College of Surgeons of England.

He did not return to Sierra Leone to practice because from 1902 the West African Medical Service was restricted to Doctors of European descent, non-white Doctors had to join a separate service as "Native Medical Officers", with a lower salary scale, in which no matter how senior or well qualified they were they were junior to the most recently qualified white Doctor. He resolutely refused to accept these degrading conditions. Otherwise it seems strange that he should have chosen to practice in England.

He was adviser for Africa at a number of Committees in the Colonial Office. He was married to Amy Hotobah-During and they were blessed with Patrice, Robert, Shola and Richard. He moved to Nottingham in the early 1950s and established a successful Medical Family Practice and served as a visiting consultant in ophthalmology at Nottingham General Hospital. He went back to Sierra Leone after many years in England with the intention of helping to establish a Medical School there. Meanwhile he had written and published his autobiography *Kossoh Town Boy* Cambridge University Press 1960 and also *An Innocent in Britain* published by Campbell Matthews & Co. Ltd., London 1988. He would later return to England where he retired and died in 1995. He was working on a Grammar of the Krio language at the time of his death.

Phoebe, a talented artist, who married Assistant Bishop Percy Jones had two children. Wilfred qualified as a physician, married Sally who was a gifted operatic singer. They settled in Canada, where Wilfred was a medical Director based in Saskatchewan. Unfortunately Wilfred died within two years of retirement in 2003, survived by his second wife Lilian and children, Veronica, Fiona, John having lost his first wife Sally.

Dr. Wilfred Jones
1934 –2003
M.B., B.S., D.P.H., F.R.C.O.G.

Mai, sister of Wilfred, qualified in Law in Nottingham, later worked in Nigeria then in New York.
Unfortunately Wilfred and Mai are no longer with us.

Eric Solomon Ageh Wellesley-Cole, (1918-1990) B.Sc., M.Inst.C.Eng. He married Ziporah Lewis. He worked most of his life in Bedford, England, and later moved to Freetown where he set up his own engineering firm. They had the following children: Ohodae, Tunde, Olivia, Wilfred, Josephine.

The following article appeared in West Africa, Current Affairs[29].

A remarkable life – Robert Wellesley-Cole, 1907-1995

Robert Benjamin Ageh Wellesley-Cole was born in Freetown, Sierra Leone, West Africa, on Monday March 11th 1907. His great, great grandfather, a Nigerian prince early in the nineteenth century, was rescued from a trans-Atlantic kidnapping, and settled as a free citizen in Freetown, the oldest British colony. He was baptised a Christian, and in the process took the name of the "greatest warrior in the world", Wellesley, Duke of Wellington, which became the family name of all the males.

He went to the Government Model School in 1914. In 1919 he became head boy and number one pupil on the register of the Secondary School which Government then started at the campus. In 1925, when Edward, Prince of Wales, visited Sierra Leone, he formally opened it in its new site, under the name of Prince of Wales School.

From there he went to the C.M.S., (later the Sierra Leone) Grammar School, where in 1922, as head boy, he passed the Cambridge Senior School Leaving Certificate in Division One with four distinctions, including Latin and Greek.

In 1924 he went to Fourah Bay College, founded by the missionaries in 1827, affiliated to Durham University in 1876, where in 1926 he obtained a degree in Mathematics and Classics, and was appointed Assistant Lecturer in Mathematics. In 1928, by study with University Correspondence College, Cambridge, he obtained an Upper Second class honours degree of London University in Philosophy.

He came to England in 1928 to obtain a Degree in Medicine, with subsequent specialisation in Surgery, at Newcastle-upon-Tyne Medical College. In the six years of training he obtained a Pass with First Class honours in every professional examination, including the only First at the finals. He also won thirteen class prizes, five specially contested prizes, plus a special postgraduate prize in Philosophy.

In 1932 he married his Scottish hostess, Anna Isabel Law Brodie of the clan of Brodie, her mother being one of the Laws of the Scottish Border, and cousin of Andrew Bonar Law, Prime Minister 1922.

In 1943 by thesis and examination he obtained the Doctorate in Medicine, M.D. of his university, and was elected a Fellow of the Royal Society of Medicine.

The following year, 1944, confronted with difficulties in passing the examination for the Fellowship of the Royal College of Surgeons in England, which no black candidate as yet had obtained, he made a three fold address at the problem of becoming a surgeon specialist. In June he sat the Master of Surgery of his university, and satisfied both home and visiting examiners, and obtained the M.S. In October he went to Edinburgh, satisfied the examiners, and was duly elected a Fellow of the Royal College of Surgeons of Edinburgh. In November he went up to London and this time satisfied the examiners and was duly elected a Fellow of the Royal College of Surgeons of England — the first member of the black race.

At the onset of the war in 1939 he applied for enlistment, but it was not answered. In those days the King's Commission was awarded to only the British subjects of "pure European descent" and so the doctor could only be listed as a captain. As a result he was available for service and responsibilities in England during the war. From 1942 to 1958 he was a Member of the

Colonial Office Advisory Committees on the Welfare of Colonial Peoples in the United Kingdom (Chairman Lord Farringdon); the Colonial Economic Development Council (Chairman Lord Portal); and the Colonial Advisory Medical Committee (Chairman Lord Listowel).

In 1945, the last year of the war, he toured the four British Colonial territories in West Africa; Gambia, Sierra Leone, Gold Coast and Nigeria from March to September, as a Member of the Advisory Committee for the Welfare of Colonial Peoples, and as a result played a key part in preventing the British Government from lowering the standard of High education, and instead raising it up to the standard and protection of London University, in particularly saving Fourah Bay College and converting it into the nucleus of a Sierra Leone University.

With the onset of the National Health Service in 1948, treatment of patients was free, and the payment was the charge of the Government, separated General Practitioners and Consultants. To be accepted as a surgeon consultant, he sold his General practice, and depended on the Nursing homes for hospital treatment of his patients. He had to find somewhere else in England to make a fresh start; and his wife, who was a generation older, and always lived in Newcastle, could not be involved in this sacrifice. They agreed to divorce in 1950. They had been together 22 years.

He found Nottingham ideal; found a friendly newly developing area where the patients were very friendly. He married that year an African student nurse, from Freetown, whose maternal grandfather was French. He quickly built a General Practice, plus a Consultant practice with his own private Nursing Home, consulting rooms and staff. Since his surgical qualifications, research interest in Eye (ophthalmic) cases, and regular visits to London on alternate weeks in Committees and other engagements, gave him interest in undergoing training at the central teaching Eye centres there, and he passed both parts of the specialist examination in Ophthalmic Medicine and Surgery by 1950. By 1960 he had published a research article on his examination and treatment of 10,000 eye patients who consulted him. By 1960 he was earning £6,000.

In 1961, he and his wife were invited to a Garden Party at Buckingham Palace, and introduced to Her Majesty and the Duke of Edinburgh at tea. The same year recently independent Nigeria invited him to a sabbatical professional visit as Senior Surgeon Specialist. Also the magistrates of Nottingham invited him to join them as Justice of Peace (the first black), on his return. He was British born, and had lived thirty three years uninterruptedly in England, as house owner, ratepayer and taxpayer.

Surprisingly, when the passports were returned to them there on British soil, they had the Expiry Date reduced to August 1962 from February 1963, "United Kingdom and Colonies citizen" changed to "Commonwealth citizen", but "Nation Status British Subject" remained unaltered.

Despite strong, numerous protests starting from 1963 for 20 years till 1982 he and his family were refused British passports; and whenever they arrived in England to resume residence, his forcibly adopted Sierra Leone passports were always classed "Visitor" and stamped "Admitted on condition that holder does not remain in the United Kingdom longer than six months".

The Wellesley Cole collection was donated to the Library of the School of Oriental and African Studies by Dr. Wellesley Cole in 1989 and in April 1991. The papers include correspondence, Colonial Office work, Nigerian material, Sierra Leone material, Memberships of Society's RWC's, scholarly work and finance. Arrangements will be made for terminal papers and other material to be placed at the hands of the archivist in the near future. Included among his published work are: *Kossoh Town Boy* (Cambridge University Press, 1960), *An Innocent in Britain* (Autobiography), (London, 1988). Unpublished are these titles; Non-fiction – *Black Paradise* (Travelogue of Africa), Fiction – *Country Doctor* and *Black Swan*.

He was also working on a Grammar of the Krio Language of Sierra Leone.

●*Material for this obituary came from the Department of Archives of the School of Oriental and African Studies, London.*

The following article appeared in West Africa, Current Affairs[30].

A life of service – Mrs. Irene E B Ighodaro 1916-1995

Doctor (Mrs.) Irene Elizabeth Beatrice Ighodaro (née Wellesley Cole), MBE, MBBS (Dunelm), FMCGP (Nigeria), Sierra Leone's first and black Africa's second female medical doctor, was born on May 16th 1916, in Freetown, Sierra Leone.

She was the fourth of six children of Wilfred and Eliza Beatrice Wellesley Cole. Her father, Wilfred Sydney Ageh Wellesley Cole, MBE, who became Superintendent of black Africa's first modern waterworks system, was West Africa's first Water Engineer. In the colonial service in Africa, he was the only black head of service for three decades. A great uncle read law at Christ Church, Oxford, (1881-1887) before qualifying as a doctor in Edinburgh in 1895; and her eldest brother, Dr. Robert Wellesley Cole, who died in October 1995 at the age of 88, was the first

Irene E B Ighodaro
M.B.E., M.B.B.S., F.M.C.G.P.

African to be elected a Fellow by examination of the Royal College of Surgeons of England, after an outstandingly brilliant career at her university. An uncle, Francis Okrafo Smart, with the aid of her father, built the City Hotel, immortalised in Graham Greene's *The Heart of the Matter*, for his client, the millionaire philanthropist, Peter J C Thomas.

Irene Ighodaro attended the Annie Walsh Memorial School, Freetown, West Africa's oldest secondary school for girls. She planned to go to Fourah Bay College to study Languages, but when her mother fell ill, Irene instead devoted herself to caring for her, though she became bed-ridden and passed away in 1933, when Irene was 16 years old. In the meantime, Dorothy Pole, her ex-headmistress offered her a job teaching French and English to the first form of AWMS, which she did for the next two years. Her brother Robert qualified as a doctor in 1934, invited her to come and study any course she wished. As she was not sure what to choose, her father advised that she study medicine. Irene embarked for England in June, 1938. She enrolled in October in the pre-medical school and one year later, at the start of the Second World War, entered the medical school of the University of Durham at Newcastle-upon-Tyne. She was the only African woman in the university.

She was involved in the war effort, manning the university telephone exchange at night, and working in a decontamination squad. As the war progressed, Newcastle experienced more air raids and the surgical and medical teams, of which she was a member, treated both wounded British soldiers and German prisoners of war. The European phase of the war ended in 1944, when she qualified.

Immediately after qualifying, she was employed as a Houseman at the Royal Victoria Infirmary, Newcastle, from August 1944, under Professor Farquhar Murray. She was next employed by her brother and, ran his large practice in Newcastle – 6,000 patients within a six-mile radius during 1945.

During the forties, she spent several holidays in London at the West African Students Union hostel (WASU), run by the late Barrister Ladipo Solanke. It was a centre of African nationalism, where students from all over West Africa studying in different British Universities, and other visiting from the USA, met and exchanged ideas. So when independence came to their countries, those who had been at WASU knew most of the students who had come to wield enormous power and influence; people like Aggrey, Hayford, Azikiwi, Wallace Johnson, Kwame Nkrumah, Mbonu Ojike, Nwafor Orizu, Ade Adedoyin, H O Davies and Obafemi Awolowo.

Irene met her husband-to-be, Samuel Osarogie Ighodaro, when he was at Fourah Bay College, Freetown, in 1936, and married in England in 1947. Mr. Ighodaro qualified as a lawyer in 1949, becoming the first Bini lawyer, and the couple returned to Benin City, Nigeria, in 1950, where she established a private practice. Her arrival changed society and its perception of the role and capability of women. There were no African doctors in Benin, and the reaction to the sight of a woman, a doctor, driving herself, in that ancient kingdom is best imagined. When she went to register to vote in Nigeria's first elections, she was at first refused on the grounds that women did not pay tax, but she insisted on paying tax and voting.

In 1952, Mr. Ighodaro became the first Minister of Health in the Western Region, and the family moved to Ibadan. Dr. Ighodaro set up a private clinic, which she ran from 1952 till 1967, when her husband was appointed a Judge of the Midwest High Court and the family moved back to Benin City. Dr. Ighodaro continued in private practice until she was in her seventies.

Dr. Ighodaro was a woman who sought every

opportunity to uplift her surroundings, even beyond her calling as a doctor. She was particularly active in working for the improvement of women everywhere and played a seminal role in the growth of many associations. She was one of four founder members, when the National Council of Women's Societies was started by Mrs. Ogunlesi and Mrs. Esan, in 1959. She was awarded the MBE in 1958.

In the mid-60s, she was Chairman of the Committee of St Brigid's Social Centre, Ibadan. The Centre, in a building provided by the Roman Catholic Church, motivated and taught married women practical skills, such as cooking, baking, sewing, budgeting, house cleaning, marketing, jewellery making, crocheting, knitting, keep-fit classes, dinner parties etc. St Brigid's also arranged for extra mural classes from the University of Ibadan, to prepare women to take the entrance exams to the University, which many passed.

Dr. Ighodaro was National President of the Young Women's Christian Association from 1965 to 1969, and World Vice-President from 1967 to 1971; she was the first National President of the Medical Women's Association of Nigeria; First National President of the Nigerian Association of University Women; one of the first Trustees, for about 20 years, of the Nigerian Medical Association, and a Foundation Fellow of the Nigerian Medical Council, to name a few of her affiliations.

She was appointed the first Chairman of the University of Benin Teaching Hospital Management Board, Benin City, with a remit to create and establish the teaching hospital. It was the first time a woman had been appointed to so high a policy-making position in Nigeria.

She consulted the contacts she had made over the years, in Ibadan, the UK, Scandinavia, the USA and Hungary, and found a huge amount of goodwill which she was able to harness. She forced the project past bureaucratic obstruction, male egos, political sabotage and vested interest and ensured that the hospital was built, staffed and opened in two years, an achievement which the then Governor, the dynamic Colonel Ogbemudia, thanked her for and rated as one of his greatest achievements. She then became first Chairman of the Board of Governors, University of Benin Teaching Hospital.

Her first book, *Baby's First Year* was published in 1966, and her autobiography, entitled *A Life of Service*, has recently been printed and is shortly to be released.

In an interview given to a Nigerian magazine in 1990, Dr. Ighodaro responded, when asked what she most enjoyed as a youth. "When is one young and when does one get old? ... I've been nearly everywhere around the world. I have been to every continent in the world. I have known the high, I have known the low. I have seen almost all the volcanoes that we read of in history. I have seen the great rivers. I have seen the Eskimos ... I have been very lucky".

Dr. Ighodaro died at home on Wednesday, 29th November 1995, at the age of 79 years. She is survived by three sons, Anthony, Wilfred and Ayodele. A daughter Oluyinka and her sister, Taiwo. Her husband having died in 1994.

10

Francis Weeks Okrafor-Smart
My Grandfather

My grandfather Francis 1874–1930 was the third child of Francis John and Mary (née Aboko-Cole).

> ### FRANCIS WEEKS OKRAFOR-SMART
> ### 1874 – 1930
>
> As part of the British Empire, which we are so glad to be; we are to begin to realise what it means to be a part of vast Empire, and what is the part we have to play in it. Certainly not the part of the helpless, spoiled, grown-up boy who would not try for himself but would always be hanging upon his parents for everything he needs. Certainly not at all. Our duty is to build ourselves into a pillar. However small at first, yet a solid and independent pillar standing upon its own base, helping with his bigger brothers and other pillars, to

> support the empire. Our first duty in this direction is to make ourselves self-dependent, self-supporting and self-governing.[31]

He was born on July 14th 1874. In line with the family history his educational journey started with school at Regent village. He would later attend the Grammar School, which he entered in 1891 and was 1458 on the register. After school he spent most of his adult life as a builder. He nevertheless had various interests in local and national matters.

On leaving school he would become a Master Builder. He trained in the Mission Diocesan Technical School under Reverend Edmonson, a distinguished Afro-West Indian. He was successful and innovative in many aspects of building.

He was a talented man with immense ideas. His singular thinking at the time seems unorthodox. His hearing disability, a common defect which affected members of the family over several generations, was not a disabling factor. His interest in matters relating to the future development of Sierra Leone is one of admiration.

His interests spread across issues such as architecture, agriculture, education, social integration and politics. He was a prolific writer and commented regularly on issues important in the future development of Sierra Leone he wrote regularly for The Sierra Leone Weekly News, later The Weekly News.

His contribution in these areas will be explored and analysed. The analysis is important, in order to illustrate the complex situation and development in Sierra Leone as seen during the period of the early decades of the 20th Century.

City Hotel - Freetown

His most impressive building in Freetown was the City Hotel. This was immortalised by Graham Greene in his novel *The Heart of the Matter*. Unfortunately, this beautifully designed building landscaped in a surrounding of tropical palms and exotic flowers was burnt down during the Civil War in the 1990s. An interesting aspect of Francis' skill as a builder was his emphasis on health and hygiene. He was keen in designing and constructing buildings with particular attention on adequate ventilation, which he recognised as healthy in the tropical climate.

An advertisement was placed in The Weekly News in 1907 entitled Health Culture. There were testimonials from Mr. P Lemberg, the Mayor of Freetown, Mr. Wilfred S Wellesley-Cole, Superintendent Water Works (brother-in-law), and Mr. W T Prout MB, CMB. They agreed that Mr. Francis W Smart was one of the best builders in the town and sure to give satisfaction to any gentleman who may require his services. It concluded, "Mr. Smart has a thorough knowledge of building construction and is one of the few scientific and reliable builders in the country."[32]

Here was a Sierra Leonean, with enormous skills and expertise, who had a successful business as a builder. At any given time he had as many as ten journeymen as trainees.

In the Sierra Leone Weekly News of 3rd November 1906 an article is published showing F W Smart as one of the Directors of The Freetown Manufacturing Company Ltd, manufacturing Hollow Concrete Building Blocks. The other members being W P Golley, J W Cole and W N Thomas.[33]

The heading of the article was "Contracts for building accepted, estimates supplied on application".

Here is the reproduction of the advert.

> # THE FREETOWN MANUFACTURING COMPANY LTD.
>
> The public is hereby notified that through the kind permission of His Excellency the Governor, we have installed our plants at the Botanical Gardens near the quarry and are ready to supply them with Hollow Concrete Building Blocks.
>
> In order to introduce the blocks to the public we have decided to give
> ## LIBERAL DISCOUNTS
> to the first ten orders received, three of which have been received and filled. Those about to build should apply to us for our quotation, thereby making some reduction in the cost of the house, and get the best house in addition. Houses built of Hollow Concrete Blocks cost less than those built of cut stones. The proof of this statement is a college now being built of Hollow Concrete Blocks.

He then went on to list other advantages, such as the health aspects that they never needed repair as they improve with age, and the SAFETY aspects as thieves could not break through the walls. He maintained that these houses constructed of Building Blocks cost less. It informed the public that catalogues were available with information of the serious advantages. It concluded by saying, "This is a progressive age. We must progress with the times."

In the same article is the following advert: [34]

> We have also decided to place twenty shares of our stock at FIVE POUNDS per share in the market, so that any who are interested, can avail themselves of this opportunity.
>
> For further particulars, apply
> (1) if in person to :
> W M Thomas Esq. – Charlotte Street
> F W Smart – Bathurst Street
> W P Golley – Fort Street
> J W Cole – Brook Street
>
> (2) If by letter to, W N Thomas Esq. Charlotte Street or F W Smart, 20 Bathurst Street.
>
> Our office is at the White House, Oxford Street, where samples of our blocks can be seen. Our works are at the quarry at the Botanical Gardens (probably site of present Pademba Road Prisons) where the blocks are being made.

Years later (1920) the following was printed in the Weekly News: [35]

> ### The Governor's Interview with builders
>
> His Excellency the Governor had an interview with builders at the Government House on Wednesday, 11th instant, and among those present were Messrs. W P Golley, J W Cole, D C Parker, F W Okrafor-Smart and Alimammy Bangura, Lumpkin. The Governor spoke of the brick kiln at Bullom and Blama as well as of the Aberdeen Creek Bridge. He would also like to see laterite stones out in quarries at contract price. The interview lasted for more than an hour.

Unfortunately nothing more was mentioned and no comments by the editorial staff.

Francis was a very astute business man. His primary aim it would appear was to help to develop the country in line with more advanced countries at that time. His business interests, and his burning desire for rapid progress within the country would eventually propel him towards an intense interest in politics.

Although still working hard as a builder the next few years would see him in the setting up of **various companies**.

He wrote:

> 'Nowadays, the wealth of other countries is not acquired by individuals merely buying and selling as we seem to think, but is made by companies utilising the natural resources of their

country, manipulating and manufacturing them into useful profitable articles and sell products among themselves and to foreign countries. Our country is rich in mineral and vegetable materials, we must learn to take advantage of them, and of the facilities of transport that the railway offers'.[36]

He envisaged Sierra Leone becoming a strong pillar of support for the Empire.[37] He strongly criticised the doctrine that people of the then colony of Sierra Leone, could not succeed in business because of our different nationalities, was false and harmful. He continued this needed to be ignored and to be relegated to the background.

'We don't seem to realise the fact however honest a body of men may be, if their business is not properly organised, their methods not intelligently and systematically conducted, that business is bound to fail' he said.

'This want of an intelligent system, want of proper organisation in business was the cause of all the failures of companies formed in this country.'

In this article he dispelled the negative assumption that we could not successfully operate a company, by naming a success story.

'There is a company now at Regent formed over sixty years ago, of all the tribes there. It is in full working order today, and not showing any signs of decay. Governed by a body of twelve directors elected for life: men of common intelligence, who have properly managed the Company'.[38]

Within his article he strongly made a case for the launching of Lumbering Trade.

In the magazine the AMERICAN INVENTOR he quoted from an article entitled "Lumbering in the North West".

The article spoke of the potential wealth awaiting development of their trade. Rightly or wrongly, he felt that it was one of those enterprises which require a small outlay of capital, yet must eventually yield large profits. He wrote about our extensive forest full of valuable timbers and concluded that we have now got a railway to facilitate the transportation to the mills, wherever erected.

His next ambitious venture in the field of commerce and finance was the launching of the Sierra Leone Transportation Company of Freetown Ltd. A column was taken up in the Weekly News dated September 1907 to launch this Company. Under "communicated", the following was published:

> In accordance with the notice published last week, a meeting was held at the house known as Frontier Office at 4.30 pm on Wednesday, the Second instant, when the purpose of the Company was fully explained by Mr. Smart, the promoter, which, briefly stated, is to collect £1000 and begin with the Fishing Industry and gradually to enlarge into Fishing and Transportation Company.

The name of the Company was therefore changed, and shall henceforth be known as The Sierra Leone Industrial and Development Company Ltd.[39]

At the conclusion of the speech it was proposed by Mr. Smart, "That this Company be called The Sierra Leone Industrial and Development Company (Ltd) with a capital of £2,500 be this day floated; and that a stock of £1,000 divided into 2000 shares of 10 shillings each be now placed on the market."

Seconded by Mr. J S Labor, The Chairman, and Mr. Wilfred S Cole and carried, the stock book was then placed on the table when 114 shares was subscribed, since increased to 121 shares.

The meeting was then adjourned till Wednesday next, the 9th instant at 12 noon, when the first call of 50% of the shares subscribed would be paid.

'The Stock Book is with Mr. Smart. Apply to him for the shares you want at No 20 Bathurst Street.'

The above illustrates the organising and business skills of my grandfather Francis. His main ambition was to promote and sustain a commercial philosophy that would be vibrant in this West African City. For the first time the potential economic growth which could evolve as a result of this new Company could be seen. Here was the nucleus of dealing in the Stock Market. Unfortunately, no further information of the progress of his idea was found. Had it been successful Sierra Leone could have been perhaps the first West African state dealing in stocks and shares, and who knows what the economic impact would have resulted in those early years.

A letter was published by Francis in the Sierra Leone Weekly News of 14th December 1907. He was a Master Builder, with two journeymen and twelve boys in training. He was ready to subscribe £20, if forty other old boys of the Grammar School were each ready to subscribe £20.[40] What was his idea for making such a suggestion? If the challenge was taken up that would have raised £820. Could that have gone towards the educating of one of the boys, at a higher level?

A close scrutiny of his many thoughts, whether to do with business, agriculture, education, social affairs and politics, truly reflected his intention on modernisation, and constitutional reforms. He had clear ideas about structures of society and he made a proposal for ongoing integration by intermarriage between the Colony and the then Protectorate people.

He gave good reasons for his suggestions:

1. The Krios were in the minority.

2. Inter-marriage would unite the elite Krios with the people of the then Protectorate.

3. Should this become a reality, it would help to create a coherent and strong population and would ensure an even pace of development throughout the country.

Such practical integration, he reasoned, could create a powerful family-based community in Sierra Leone with genuine stake in the region.

Interestingly, there was an Editorial Comment in the Sierra Leone Weekly News dated Saturday September 8th 1928, entitled "Will The Sierra Leoneans (Colony Born) Die Out?"

The article went at great length to advocate exactly what Francis wrote about in 1907, the need for widespread intermarriage between the Krios and people from the Protectorate. The editorial inter alia went on: "The Sierra Leone of the future then which we envisage is one in which the various elements of Temne, Susu, Limba, Sherbro Mendi etc. will become conglomerated into one after the type of Sierra Leoneans." It continued "As an earnest of this we see the whole of the Protectorate at present interspersed with Sierra Leoneans (Colony Born) drawn either by trade; and in the Colony proper there is going to be a continuous process of assimilation through intermarriage, education and other social factors".[41]

The good news is that nearly a hundred years later this is now a welcome common practice. What foresight my grandfather Francis had!!!

He was a regular contributor on various topics, to the Sierra Leone Weekly News. While he originally accepted Sierra Leone's role as part of the British Empire, he was by no means an imperialist. In an article in August 1907, he stressed the importance of building Sierra Leone into a powerful nation, which should become a strong pillar to support the Empire.[42]

Yet in 1910, he wrote an article in which he attacked British Imperialism. By this time he was demanding independence, accusing the British Government of holding it back, because of selfish reasons. He went on in the article as far as to propose a revolution to obtain independence. He wrote, "We hold it as a self-evident truth that every country should govern itself. Foreign rule destroys the physical, intellectual and moral facilities of a people and reduces them to the level of brutes."

Article written under pen name of F W O'Krafu

ENGLANDS CATTLE FARM[43]

A cow will ordinarily live for fifteen to twenty years, but so heavy is the strain of milking that they always break down within five years. They are milked to death. Should any cow attempt to suckle herself she is speedily killed. In the same way, all these Colonies are kept not for love of the natives, but to drain them of their national wealth, and to rob them and exploit them. India, Egypt, Sierra Leone and all the Colonies in the West and on the East Coast of Africa and elsewhere, are England's Cattle Farm. The milking pays prodigiously. The English gentry grow rich thereat, and the natives grow poorer and poorer.

The Government of these countries are the most expensive in the world. They furnish lucrative posts for the English gentry who might not otherwise be able to earn a living; high salaries to Europeans, and beggarly pay to African officials are the rule.

All these Colonies, India, Egypt, Sierra Leone Lagos and the rest of them, were once great manufacturing countries. The English have destroyed manufacturers. They do it (1) by inducing the people to bring their manufactured articles into an exhibition.

These are then collected and carried to Europe for samples for which cheap and worthless imitations are made in quantities and palmed upon the helpless people, (2) and by so adjusting the taxes and duties as to make these Colonies excellent markets for the made stuff of Manchester, Leeds and Sheffield.

When an English man says we are running these Colonies to prepare the natives for self-government he lies and he knows it. The best way to learn to do a thing is to begin to do it. So the best way to learn self-government is to begin to govern self. But no. They are keeping these Colonies as they keep their Cattle Farms. More it is as a gang of armed robbers attacking a way-faring man, held him down by the gun and all his companions robbing him of his goods.

But men are not cows while England makes her Cattle Farms, these Colonies pay by exhausting the soil, there are signs that it has exhausted also the patience of a long suffering people.

EVERY COUNTRY MUST GOVERN ITSELF

1. We hold it as a self evident truth that every country should govern itself. Foreign rule destroys the physical, intellectual and moral families of a people, and reduces them to a level of brutes.

2. We hold that an enslaved people must pass through three stages, before it can again establish itself as a member of the society of nations.

3. Every race that has lost the control of its affairs must be suffering from some terrible mental and moral weakness. Foreign rule is a symptom of social decay and disorder as fever is a symptom of internal derangement

within the human system. Hence the first stage in the struggle for freedom is that of

(A) MORAL INTELLECTUAL AND INDUSTRIAL PREPARATION

During this period, we the workers, must elevate the character of the people, and instruct them to the "principles that govern an efficient social organisation". The heart of the people must be purified and higher intervals must be cut at its root, and the people must be taught to give their attention to matters pertaining to the national well-being, with the same degree of earnestness, as they do to secure their individual comforts. The spirit of the slave must disappear; the spirit of freedom be born. A knowledge of history, of politics, and of sociology must be implanted to the nation, that it may see its condition and appreciate its duties. Technical and industrial knowledge must be widely acquired, agriculture and manufacturing industries be established on modern lines. In a word, "virtue and wisdom" must be supplied to our feeble and degraded social system; in an abundant measure. "Virtue and wisdom" are the sustaining forces of society and if a nation is enslaved it must be sadly "wanting in these elements of social strength".

The spiritual qualities of virtue and wisdom must be cultivated in a high degree by the people, that our social organisations may be highly strengthened.

Literature, bands of writers and preachers, schools like those of Professor S Ferrier of Barcelona.

Demonstrations, self-sacrificing labours and other devices must be employed for the furtherance of this part of the work. The future of the movement depends on the thoroughness with which this fundamental preparation has been carried out. This first stage is the basics of the "Edifice of Liberty", and this building can only be erected on a wide and deep foundation.

(B) THE SECOND STAGE IS THAT OF WAR

A rigorous boycott, and a bloody war. The refusal to buy goods of foreign markets and good shooting are the things that will help people quickly to understand their responsible duties.

The way must be cleared for the establishment of a free and sovereign state, managed by the people and for the people.

The debris of the old regime must be removed. The only agent that can accomplish this is the sword and gun. No subject nation can win freedom without war.

He who tells the people that this is wrong, is either a fool or a knave.

(C) AFTER THE WAR, THE WORTH OF RECONSTRUCTION, AND COLSOLIDATION COMMENCE

These tasks require the exercise of the greatest qualities of statesmanship. The whole machinery of a new state has to be set up. Efficient safeguards against future dangers have to be found. Memorials of the War of Independence have to be established. The recognition of the neighbouring nations has to be obtained for the new born state. All those difficulties can be solved only by men possessing virtue and wisdom in their highest forms. "Ardent Patriots" and "Consummate Statesmen" led the nation to the promised land of freedom, after its march through the wilderness of war and suffering.

These three stages, have been passed and must be passed through by every independent nation. History says so. Even so, it must be for us.

Virtue and wisdom first, then boycott and war, finally independence.

This is our programme in a nutshell. We shall not dilate upon it on this occasion. Future articles will be devoted to practical methods for going through the first stage and laying the foundation of our national independence – we must insist on individual "Moral Progress", "Intellectual Enlightenment" and "Industrial and Agricultural pursuits". We shall bid men prepare for the war that must come. We shall ask them to be ready for the onerous duties that will have to be discharged after the triumph for the cause in the field.

Propaganda and suffering at the beginning, heroism and valour in the middle, wisdom and constructive genius at the end. This is the plan. This the only road to liberty. Whoever pretends to find a short cut is a quack and a lair. Awake! Oh Sierra Leone and West Africa!! Awake and take your place among the nations of the world.

We solicit the brotherly co-operation of all

Africans in particular, all our brother men in general. In the holy work of raising the moral, intellectual and industrial level of a large part of human race, that it may be fit to enter the temple of liberty through the gates of war.

Oh our Father, Thou that dwellest
In the High and Holy place
Thou Eternal benefactor
Of the entire Human race.

May we see our duties clearly?
And perform them one by one
And may Wisdom give us guidance
Till our earthly work is done.

Personally I think that this article carried with it an "inflammatory" tone, which was quite extraordinary, so utterly different from what normally appeared in the Sierra Leone Weekly News. The customary tone in that period was one of resignation, even despair (see pp 618-9 a History of Sierra Leone by Christopher Fyfe) not any call to war against the government.

I do not think for one moment that it represents the voice of any existing political movement in Freetown. My impression of it is that it is a précis of some book or pamphlet he had been reading. The way it is set out in sub-headings and stages, the systematic outline of a specific plan of revolutionary action it calls for, the reference to "Professor S Ferrier of Barcelona", reads to me as the work of an experienced political pamphleteer, into which Francis introduced the name of Sierra Leone.

In an Editorial comment of Sierra Leone Weekly News under Mr. Okrafor's Communication dated February 5th 1910, his article was condemned and criticised.

We published in the article of Mr. Okrafor in our issue of January 2nd not that we considered that it represented the views of the educated and responsible people of Sierra Leone, on the contrary we have every reason to know that the educated and responsible section of the Sierra Leone community utterly and entirely repudiate all the sentiments contained in that article. We published it simply and solely to show what erratic and irrational ideas find their way in the minds of some of our people.

An African who has learnt English enough to write that article, who has lived all his life in this community of Sierra Leone, where the education we have enjoyed has been brought to us by English Missionaries; where the mechanical arts and crafts including the one he practices himself, and by means of which he earns his living have been taught to us by the English Missionaries and their secular agents; where the industries and commerce of the place have been developed under the leadership of Englishmen who have provided opportunities of employment for thousands of Sierra Leoneans; where the opening up of the country and the building of the Sierra Leone Government Railway have only been practicable because Sierra Leone is an integral portion of the British Empire; that any man should live in Sierra

Leone and witness these things all his life, and every day of his life and yet has not learned to value highly the connections of Sierra Leone with the British Empire and the advantages conferred upon Sierra Leone by that connection, is certainly one of the extreme exhibitions of human blindness to what is and has always been the best interest of Sierra Leone and its population.44

A very interesting response by the Editor of Sierra Leone Weekly News on the article by Okrafor (F W O'krafu – pen name).

Social/cultural changes

The questions that must be asked are: (1) Why did he support such revolutionary actions? (2) Why did he decide to publish in the widely circulated Sierra Leone Weekly News? Events in Sierra Leone over the last twenty years at least whereby the influence, or power of the Creoles have been gradually and systematically eroded, needed to be examined.

An appropriate reference could be found in the book "An African Victorian Feminist" Life and Times of Adelaide Smith Cesely Hayford 1868 -1960 by Adelaide M Cromwell. On page 12 she writes:

'Porter refers to the period of the 1870s as the apogee of Creole ascendancy. But perhaps the most unfortunate consequence of the economic, political and social control with colonialism here, exercised by the British, was the cultural, psychological and social dependency it created. Yet evidence suggests that for this, Creoles, at least until the 1890s, there continued to be more or less willing. Acceptance of British values giving a richness and vibrancy to their life and culture which would have gladdened the hearts of the founders. This was their Golden Age, and so it might have continued if not indefinitely, for some considerable time, perhaps until the First World War had not some other changes occurred.' [45] She continues 'Both of these changes took place under the administration of Colonel Frederic Cardew, a former soldier in the Zulu Wars, who came to the colony in 1894. In order to raise funds for the transforming of the then Protectorate, he introduced the Hut Tax that led to a brutal war in which many Europeans (Missionaries) and many Creoles were killed under the leaders of Bai Bureh. Cardew felt that the Creoles by inciting the Africans not to pay the tax and by fermenting disloyalty in the press were in fact more supportive of the "native peoples" than of the Government. Therefore he set about diminishing the administration authority of the Creoles. He asked that every European Head of a Department have a European, not a Creole, Assistant. Governor Hennessy had in the early 1870s at the peak of the Creole ascendancy requested the opposite – that every European Head of Department have a Creole Assistant.'

This action which was implemented would lead to disastrous consequences and some unpleasant incidents later in Freetown. In the early years of the 1900s, there were examples of qualified Doctors not given the appropriate appointment for which they were qualified to work in.[46]

What Adelaide Cromwell describes is something far more fundamental than Cardew's policy in Sierra Leone. From the 1890s the British government inaugurated a policy of white racial rule which was introduced throughout the entire British Empire (and the other imperial powers did the same in their empires) to ensure that no non-white was in a position to have authority over a white. So in 1902 a West African Medical Service was started which was explicitly limited to those of European descent. Non-white doctors had to join a separate service as "Native Medical Officers" with a lower salary scale, in which, no matter how senior or well-qualified they were, they were junior to even the most newly qualified white doctor.

A prominent Sierra Leonean Doctor returning home in 1913 after qualifying in medicine and surgery in St Mary's Hospital, London, was refused a post in the West African Medical Service because of his colour. There were two categories of doctors – European in the "Colonial Service" and Africans in the "Local Service". As we have already seen, it was this regulation that made Dr Robert Wellesley-Cole decide to practice in England. Thus it was clear that life in Freetown in both the social and professional spheres was unpleasant and by the early years of the 1900s people were beginning to dream of Sierra Leone becoming an independent state.

Francis' "England Cattle Farm" was to a great extent a confrontational publication. As could be seen in the reproduced article he argued that "Every Country must Govern Itself". He articulated on the "Moral and Intellectual and Industrial Preparation". He then went on to the mechanism which he described under the heading of "The Second Stage is that of War", then perhaps the most powerful and rousing section of the article which was headed "After the War, The Worth of Reconstruction and Consolidation".

Interestingly, in his article, he concluded, "This is our programme in a nutshell." Why describe articles as "our programme"? Was this an indication that there was a pressure group for independence of Sierra Leone in Freetown? Did the article represent the voice of any political movement in Freetown?

It remains, however, interesting that Francis, a respectable, successful professional, should have had these revolutionary ideas and should have been ready to publish them.

In 1907 he had written an article published in the Weekly News, calling for the establishment of a Parliament or a two-tier chamber House of Representatives. His dream was for this body to be composed of two chambers – The Commons and The Lords. The Lords should be comprised of members of the present Government. The Commons should be comprised of the Representatives of every section of the Colony, i.e. the city and every village. People for the Protectorate must be represented. He envisaged a total number of 150 to 800.

He wrote

'Emphasis should be placed on what the people wanted, the things that are good for Public Welfare, Social Welfare. Ensure the property of the nation. Although priority should be the development of the country's resources which eventually would benefit all concerned.

'He put forward the need to have some policies for the wide implementation of agriculture. He thought Sierra Leone needed to build and sustain a vibrant economy invest in the manufacturing and creative spheres that would bring about wealth to the country. To his way of thinking a House of Representatives should be the nucleus for achieving these developments'.[47]

One can construe these recommendations as impracticable but nevertheless here was someone very creative in his thinking with definite objectives for the building of a nation. The fact that he was prepared to publish these thoughts, very bold indeed for the period, should be highly commended.

In January 1908 he wrote an article published in the Weekly News. The article focused on the building of Nationhood, the creation of strong economic structures based on producing, marketing our own goods, having a say on how the country was governed. In a way demanding self-government. This article exposed a burning desire for independence and one must question whether there were plans by certain groups to destabilise the country.[48]

Throughout the remaining years of his lifetime, he continued to be involved with various issues, be it in the social, religious, education or political areas. He always, whenever he could, tried to stimulate the public's reaction to burning topics of the day. One particular subject, that would stimulate much debate was the proposed introduction in Sierra Leone of the Criminal Code 1918-20. What was this Criminal Code all about?

Criminal Code

When the British Colonies were founded, the English Legal System was introduced, based on the principles of English Common Law which allows the Judges to interpret their decisions with reference to previous precedents. This system, which allows flexibility in the interpretation of the law and demands a large, experienced judiciary, was felt to be unsuitable for the Indian Sub-Continent. Instead the Government introduced a Criminal Code modelled on the "Code Napoleon", first introduced by the Emperor Napoleon, and adopted and still used by all the countries of continental Europe.

Under this system all criminal offences are listed in the Code with an appropriate penalty for each. Judges have then to decide which of the offences listed most nearly fits the case they are trying and judge accordingly.

There was talk of introducing the system into Sierra Leone where the government always tended to resent the way in which the flexibility of the Common Law system sometimes enabled the courts to give verdicts that went against official views. Obviously the proposal alarmed the Krios, who had always seen the law courts as one of the guardians of their liberty – this horrified the Freetown bar.

A large section of the Freetown public wrote constantly and published in the Weekly News their opposition to the Criminal Code becoming law. Many of these were Sierra Leonean lawyers, including some of the most successful. An example was a letter published by C D Hotobah-During, in the Weekly News dated 14th January 1920. He considered it a retrograde step which would surely prove dangerous and disastrous to the inhabitants of the Colony and Protectorate.

Francis in his letter of 13th December 1919 on the Criminal Code, in reply called for Sierra Leoneans "To sleep with one eye open". He continued, "This should be our motto henceforth; Sierra Leone has no time now to sleep soundly."[49]

The proposal was eventually dropped. However, on January 25th 1930 there appeared again the issue of the Criminal Code under the Editorial column:

> ## A CRIMINAL CODE
>
> Twelve years have rolled since Governor Wilkinson proposed the introduction of A Criminal Code for the Colony of Sierra Leone. The proposal brought together a committee which vigorously and successfully opposed the ideas as inimical to the interest of the people. Any attempt to introduce such a code will certainly revive the same if not greater opposition and will leave in its trail bitterness and mistrust between the Governor and the people, and for this sake if for no other we trust the suggestion will be discountenanced as likely to interfere with the peace and harmony of the administration.
>
> There is already in hand a large sum of money which was collected for the purpose of taking every constitutional step to oppose the project, and we have no doubt this amount will be utilised to combat any attempt at a Criminal Code in Sierra Leone, and we are quite satisfied with the present state of our law. If anything is needed it is only to make applicable some of the English Statutes after 1880; for we understand our Criminal Statutory Law goes no further than that. When that is done everything that is needful, would have been done. But a Code is most unnecessary and undesirable.

The proposal to adopt a Criminal Code – and throughout these years there was a definite 'No' against the code – was taken so seriously that the debate went on for a number of years.[50] Francis Okrafor-Smart became involved in the debate as has been illustrated.

His interest in politics was maintained throughout the rest of his short life 1874 – 1930.

On September 29th 1923, the National Congress of British West Africa (Sierra Leone Branch) held an election of its Executive Body. The Honourable Secretary of the Sierra Leone Section was Wilfred Sidney Wellesley-Cole, brother-in-law of Francis. Officers elected were:

President	Hon. C May MLC
Vice Presidents	A E Tuboku Metzger MA, JP
	J B Roberts Esq. JP, VJ
	Alimamy O Jambiria JP
Secretary	W S Cole Esq. M.Inst. M & C Eng. (Brother-in-law)
Assistant Secretaries	T E Nelson-Williams Esq. MA, BCG
	Reverend A Johnson MA, DTH
Financial Secretary	Ed E Johnson Esq.
Treasurer	B W Davies
Auditors	J A Songo Davies Esq JP
	G Eleady Cole Esq.
Unofficial members of Executive Committee	Alhaj Sabid Savage Esq., Iman of Fourah Bay
	Woman Sain Hd Deen, Iman of Freetown
	Alimamy Sort Tribal Ruler of Temnes
	George Cummngs Tribal Ruler of Mendis
	Alimamy Fafaroh Tribal Ruler of Mandigoes
	Alimany Aliu Kamara Tribal Ruler of Sisus
	Alimamy Mark Tribal Ruler of Limbas
	Alimamy Kangbe Tribal Ruler of Lokkohs
	Alimany Mahomet Kamera Tribal Ruler of Sarakulis

John Lewis Esq.
Reverend O E Taylor
Reverend B L Thomas MA, LTH
E A Ejesa Osora MA
J E Leigh
T C John MA
J G Wilson
Professor O Faduma BDPhD
Dr. J A Williams MN, ChB
Dr. H C Bankole-Bright LRCP, LRCS etc.
J Jenkins-Johnson
T C Woode MPS
C W Betts
J Nelson-Williams
E S Beoku-Betts, MA, ELL, LLB
F A Miller JP
C J R Thomas
Dan J Edwin
Alex D Yaskey
F W Okrafo-Smart
G M Spilsbury
M D Lucas NJPM Boston BA, Barrister-at-law
H A Morrison
E L Auber JP
C A Innis
D E Carney
J I Benjamin
Three vacancies to be filled

W S Cole
Hon Secretary Sierra Leone Section
NCBW[51]

The membership of the Sierra Leone Branch is a good reflection of representatives of the various professional and ethnic mix at the time. They were speaking with one voice, thereby reflecting a strong bond and cohesion for the political advancement of Sierra Leone.

The descendants of some of the above members at some period or the other have participated in various fields covering education, medical, legal and business advancement in the country. It is imperative to emphasize that some of their ancestors were Liberated Africans and settlers (Nova-Scotia) people who were rescued and resettled in Freetown from 1787 to about 1860.

Ancestors of Francis Okrafor-Smart have been involved in the specific areas of education and religion. Francis' interests covered a wide variety of areas. One of which was his interest politics.

Why National Congress of British West Africa?

'It is one of the ironies of colonialism that the time when the Imperial Power Britain, was engaged in a titanic struggle with Wilhelmine Germany, her African subjects made no overt attempt to overthrow her rule. This is not to say that they did not have reasons enough to.... There were faint rumblings of political challenge.'[52]

Dr. J K Randle, a Sierra Leone resident in Lagos, had this to say:

> 'The fact must, however, not be disguised even here that in recent years the administration of the Government of this Colony has not given the people entire satisfaction… The people see that government is not carried in their interest. But, however painfully true this is, let us not forget the wider principle that we are citizens of the British Empire.'[53]

The Krio society on the whole had strong feelings of attachment to the causes of the Empire, and Sierra Leone as a member of the British Empire, had supported the war and prepared to offer their lives on behalf of their King and England.

Things began to go sour at the way Africans were being ill-treated after the war. Akintola Wyse observes:

> "Moreover, the war, primarily a European conflict, caused a great deal of dislocation and economic distress".[54]

Interesting to note that Francis Okrafor-Smart had on various occasions put forward ideas for political, educational and economic advancement. He wrote about; "the importance of building ourselves into a strong nation, becoming a strong pillar to support the Empire" in the Weekly News in 1907.

Francis continued to do very well in his main occupation as a builder, this included churches and some elegant buildings in Freetown, amongst which is the Chanrai building in what was Wilberforce Street. He also maintained his interest in agriculture. He criticised the school system for teaching "words, words, words". He wrote, "They require a sound knowledge of agriculture, and many other useful arts."[55]

In the same article, he agonised on the lack of interest of the public in general for not "turning their hands to the land". He wrote:

> 'Our grandfathers brought the knowledge of agriculture with them (meaning the Liberated Africans). They made farms and planted orchards. Almost all the fruit trees now in the colony were planted by them. Their children were sent to school to learn "book".
>
> 'In due time, these parents died, leaving the land and orchards to their children. Because they were not taught farming, the land was left to grow wild and is now out of control. Therefore delicate plants such as bananas and plantains have disappeared from the colony. Many others such as oranges and pears have ceased bearing altogether.'

As a statement to his interest in agriculture Francis would embark on what could be described as his biggest venture or project. In 1911 he purchased a large acreage of land at George Brook, which would become a showpiece of an agricultural farm, where various tropical fruits would be cultivated and grown. He called his farm at George Brook "Fine Waters at St George's Valley" later to be known as Smart Farm.

The legal documents for the sale of land were drawn up on the 23rd of March 1911 between —

> Ebenezar Lancelot Auber of Bathurst Street, Freetown, Sierra Leone, city bailiff and Richard Temple of Robert Street, Freetown, Sierra Leone, Mercantile Clerk of the one part and Francis Simeon Weeks Okrafor-Smart of Bathurst Street aforesaid builder of the other part… Use of the said Francis Weeks Okrafor-Smart his heirs and assignees forever.

Signed and dated 23rd March 1911. Over the years from 1911, Francis would buy surrounding acres of land and by doing this his farm became quite extensive. Smart Farm was well known and very popular because of the various fruits such as mangoes, oranges, clementines, bananas, breadfruit, pawpaw, pears, different types of plums, pineapples, guava, sugar cane. Most impressive was the swimming pool which was very popular indeed. This was opened to the public and for a charge of two pence one could swim as long as one wanted.

Grandfather as a builder built a very attractive ferro-concrete house. This was a three-story house with a veranda on the second and third floors. There were five bedrooms, a large dining room, an inside kitchen with an Aga-type wood-burning cooker with four plates, hot water reservoir and oven. From the back of which an eight inch diameter circular chimney of beaten iron sheets passed right up the wall to pierce the eaves of the roof – see photo of OkraforVille.

As a child I remember many happy days growing up in such opulent surroundings.

OkraforVille – Smart Farm

On bank holidays various groups would come to Smart Farm for a day out for picnics, to enjoy the swimming pool, or just to enjoy the countryside. Of course there was the "Brook", a range of varieties of plants and trees and tropical wild flowers. My sisters and brothers used to enjoy inviting their friends to Smart Farm. Very happy days they were. As time went by Francis started to cultivate edible agricultural items such as cassava and even kept pigs. Thereby developing his farm as a mixed farming enterprise.

He published an article in the Sierra Leone Weekly News on the 11th April 1925 to announce his discovery of a certain type of fertiliser.

NOTES ON AGRICULTURE
by W. O'krafor Smart

The Warapa Bengal Bean or Velvet Bean. In the practice of agriculture in this country, our soils are found to be very poor, and crops do not yield well. After planting our staple crops such as cassada or ginger or rice once or twice, the land has to be left for a number of years to grow up to bush. Fresh land is cleared only to be left after farming it for a year or two to clear again still another land.

This condition of things makes farming very laborious: fresh land has to be cleared every year, makes the cost of producing crops very high, and farming very unprofitable.

WELL WHAT IS TO BE DONE? In the meanwhile the demand for food is growing more and more intense. Food is not cheap and there is the English market calling on us louder and louder to supply it with cotton, ginger, coffee, starch, banana, and comet tomato. Yet all these things, and more, are easily produced in this county, if only the land can be brought to a high state of production, within a short space of time, and at a little extra cost of labour, and this – the writer is very, very glad to inform all those who farm or intend to farm – is now attainable. This is to say, by the new method now being introduced, you can plant your ginger, cotton or casssada year after year on the same land, the yield instead of steadily declining, will be either maintained or increased – according to the method used in harvesting the crops which will be explained later.

AN ACCIDENTAL DISCOVERY.

This statement is not made lightly. You know O'krafor Smart always write earnestly: and his published ideas always bring good results. You will remember the article of 1910 for the introduction of Concrete Block Buildings into this country; and as a result of that article, the face of the city of Freetown is today completely changed.

Today a new system of farming is about to be introduced which will enable us to make larger and larger farms, and at less cost, and make the crops increase more and more every year – farming the same land. This statement is made possible because of study and accidental discovery.

THE WARAPA. The means by which this wonderful change will be obtained is by the extensive use of that lowly and despised plant, called the Warapa in Sierra Leone, Bengal Bean in England, Velvet bean in America.

The poor condition of our soil mentioned in the beginning of this article is not peculiar to us. It is a common condition in Tropical and sub-Tropical countries all over the world, and the American Government has long been studying how to improve this kind of soil: and after searching for a long time by practice and experiment, it has found that the Velvet Bean or Warapa is the best plant known to many today which can bring a poor land to high state of production at the lowest possible cost, and at the shortest possible time.

Says Professor M A Crosley in Farm Practices that increase crops yields, page 11:

"The Velvet Bean – Warapa – unquestionably heads the list of crops that may be used for soil improvement. It will succeed in practically all soils of this region. The Southern States by the Gulf of Mexico – makes a good growth on poor land, and produces a greater amount of vegetable matter to be returned to the soil than any other crops suitable to this region. In addition it is one of the best grazing crops that can be had for cattle and hogs in the dry season and is also a good money crop when grown for seed, or to be ground into velvet bean meal for feeding to hogs. The Velvet Bean – Warapa – therefore serves a double purpose in that, if it is properly utilized it will greatly increase the farm income and greatly improve the soil at the same time.

Over most of this section, this crop should be the principle reliance for building up the soil, as it is easy and inexpensive to grow and produces quicker results than any other crops adapted to the soils and climate condition of this section.

It is always advisable to plant it with some crop, and to secure the full benefit of the Warapa, enough live stock — cows, goats, hogs should be kept to graze off the vines after the interplanted crops such as corn or cassada has been harvested.

When Warapa is grazed off in this manner, practically all the fertilizing material in the crops is returned to the soil.

At the price of commercial nitrogen in 1918, a good crop of Warapa will supply about £10 worth of this valuable element of plant food per acre.

This gives some idea of the immense value this crop has as a means of maintaining and increasing crop yields".

Modern farm practice has found out that the best way to improve land is by intercropping with legumes such as Warapa and twin beans: Congo Beans, etc. And the Warapa has been found to be the best of them all.

It has also been found that for soil improvement, Warapa can be grown on the same land year after year; and that it troubles the interplanted crops but little. And it is just here that the writer's accidental discovery comes in, which is that when planted with root crops such as cassava, yams, and possibly ginger and all other root crops, it actually makes those plants shaded and entangled by it bear better than those away from it.

This though a small discovery is of very great value. Farmers need not hesitate to plant the Warapa with their cassava, yams or ginger fearing it will humbug them so they will not bear. Remember — it will make those plants shaded and entangled by it, bear better than those away from it; and next year the plants will bear the same or better plants than this year.

Plant it in distances of six feet. If it is an old farm put one milk cup full white lime on the heap. If there is no lime, use ashes. Ashes contain about sixty-six per cent of lime. Lime all the land once in four years, when there is money to do it at the rate of 1,000 to 2,000 lbs per acre, and that is all.

When that is done it will do the following:- (1) Make those plants shaded and entangled bear better than the others; (2) It will put nitrogen in the soil worth about £10 per acre and make it grow richer and richer the oftener it is planted; (3) It will yield seed that is eaten by men though for a small extent, but chiefly used for feeding hogs.

In Florida, the ration for a hog weighing 100 pounds or for a brood sow is as follows.

One pound Warapa seed, ground seed and pod together, one-half pound corn ground, mixed in one gallon of water and soaked for twenty-four hours. Use cassada instead of corn; use one pound foofoo and one pound Warapa seed. Grind the seed with the pod, add the foofoo mix them in one gallon of water and soak for twenty-four house before feeding. The Warapa yields 1,000 to 1,500 lbs of seed per acre. Therefore it helps to make hog raising easy and profitable. (4) It will enable you to use the land continually: this means that you can keep larger and larger farms by increasing the area yearly. The yield of crops is maintained or increased according to the method using in harvesting. (5) It enables you to raise cows easily; you tie the cow where cassava has been harvested; the cow will eat the vines, and by trampling the rest under foot makes the land yield better when next it is planted. One acre of warapa will maintain a cow and two hogs for five months.

No other single crops will do all the five points mentioned above so well, so quickly and so cheaply as the warapa.

The United States Government advised the farmers to plant two-thirds of their land every year to warapa interplanted with corn and ground nut. The remaining third being planted to cotton, in which case twin beans is recommended to be planted with the cotton. That is to say all the land is to be interplanted with some legume every year.

If cotton is being planted, that is the plan to follow. If not, then plant warapa with all other crops planted: cassava, koko, yams, ginger, corn or groundnut.

Plant Warapa! Plant Warapa!! Plant Warapa!!!

That is the *key* to profitable *farming*.[56]

A Farmer from Nigeria responded and expressed an interest having read the article in the Weekly News. Francis replied and promised to send samples.

12 Can Lane
Lagos,
26th June 1925

Dear Sir,

Your contribution to the Sierra Leone WEEKLY NEWS of 11th April in regards to your discovery of Warapa plant as soil fertilizer has attracted my attention.

Indeed the method which obtains in Sierra Leone to allow used up farmlands to lie fallow for several years, in order to improve the soil is the common practice in Nigeria and neighbouring countries; and as clearly pointed out in your article it does make farming laborious and expensive.

Your statement that the discovery of the plant was accidental can hardly be correct as nothing happens accidentally in this mundane world of ours, and if you believe and I am sure you do, the Biblical statement that not a sparrow falleth without the knowledge of the Grand Geometrician of the Universe, you will agree with me that the use of the word was incorrect; it is a misnomer and should not have found expression in human language. The time for the discovery and for the discovered of the Warapa plant was due when you found and published it for general information – an indication that you are an instrument in God's Hands to remedy the deplorable state of farming not only in Sierra Leone but in West Africa – a long felt desideratum.

However, I withhold at present my congratulations to you for the discovery of this plant until its utility as detailed by you has been proved. But I would readily convey my thanks to you for the light you have unselfishly thrown on this most important branch of our industrial work – the be-all of the Negro Race.

I have no doubt that the Warapa and other plants mentioned in your article are indigenous to Nigerian soil, but evidently unknown amongst legumes as possessing such rare qualities.

I am therefore asking you kindly to send me some sound Warapa beans for a trial – a favour I trust you will not deny me – and for which I enclose herewith Postal Order for 2s. 6d. to defray cost and postage of the beans; the parcel should be registered to ensure delivery at this end.

May I ask please to what extent does the Warapa plant affect the wild undergrowth as it spreads over the soil?

With assurance of my best wishes I remain, – yours sincerely,

C. IDARE AKINSAN

This letter was written to F. Okrafo Smart, Esq., C/o Editor Sierra Leone Weekly News, Oxford Street, Freetown, Sierra Leone[57]

In his reply F Okrafo Smart wrote,

Dear Mr. Akinsan,

Your interesting letter of June 26th was duly handed by the WEEKLY NEWS and the contents have been carefully noted.

I thank you very much for your kind letter and the sentiments contained therein.

Two days previous to the receipt of this letter, a gentleman had made just the same expression to me about the possibility of my being an instrument in God's hands to remedy the deplorable state of farming not only in Sierra Leone but in West Africa – a long felt *desideratum*.

As to me, I feel that God has given me something for the people in the lines indicated and my daily prayer is for Grace and Power to lay it before them. And for help in its realisation by actual practice.

As to proving the utility of the Warapa plant or Indian Warapa plant as it will henceforth be called according to the suggestion of the Honourable M. T. Dawe, M.B.E. Commissioner of Lands and Forest; to distinguish its the non-stirging from the stirging Warapa that has been settled long long ago; all that remains for us to do is to learn to use it efficiently just as one buys a motor car and learns to use it – the experimental stage in both cases having been long past.

As to what extent the plant affects the wild undergrowth as it spreads over the soil?

In cultivated fields, it keeps down and smothers all weeds and other grasses that generally starts late in the season amongst cultivated crops, making further cultivation unnecessary. And in addition it makes the interplanted crop, if a root crop, bear better.

The beans requested are sent you herewith by registered post as advised. And I trust it will reach you in good condition. Although the season is far advanced, if planted now in good soil, it will grow and bear some seeds for your next year's planting; Yours very truly,

F. OKRAFO SMART[58]

In the Weekly News of 8th August 1925 he invited the public to his farm to witness the actual plants and beans[59]:

NOTES ON AGRICULTURE

To the Editor of the WEEKLY NEWS

Sir, Because they contain matters of some interest to the people, I shall be glad if you will kindly publish the enclosed letter and reply in your next issue.

It will also prove useful if you will kindly publish the other articles on the subject of the Warapa or Indian Warapa as it will henceforth be called, for it will benefit those readers who may not have seen it elsewhere as well as afford the opportunity to others to reread them again, this time more carefully especially so, now that the Hon. M. T. Dawe, O.B.E., Commissioner of Lands and Forests has confirmed the fact that the cultivation of the plant should be encouraged.

I wish to add also that there are some of the beans still on hand for free distribution, and to state that anyone who wants to see Indian Warapa actually growing and bearing may come to the farm Fine Waters at St. George's Valley, on Wednesday, Fridays and Saturdays, afternoons only – when it will be my pleasure so show the plant with the pods hanging on it.

When one considers the value of this plant (1) to the cow and goats for milk production, (2) to the pigs for pork (3) to the land for nitrogen and (4) to the farmer himself for food and money, it is to be hoped that widespread interest will be taken in its cultivation and use.

F. W. OKRAFO SMART

The above description conveys a farming enterprise that was productive and successful. Unfortunately Smart Farm lost its attraction and beauty and over the years, due to unfortunate circumstances, it is now nothing but a huge housing estate. Very sad indeed.

Regent Centenary Celebrations
9th - 17th November 1913

Medal to Commemorate the Centenary
Celebrations of Regent Village
1813-1913
Picture on right shows St Charles' Parish Church

'The celebrations of the Centenary of the establishment of the village of Regent were observed throughout the week by a high demonstration at which nearly every important citizen took part. The programme was elaborately conceived and carefully carried out under the direction of a Committee presided over by J W Whitfield Esq. as chairman, and Dr. Randle as Master of Ceremonies. The secretaries were Reverend N H Boston M.A., and S A Macauley Esq. A large number of visitors from various parts poured throughout the week into the village. His Excellency the Acting Governor honoured the occasion by his presence accompanied by his A.D.C. and the Commissioner of Police. The celebrations were eminently successful.'[60]

One of the notable participants in the above celebrations was Francis Okrafor Smart. On Monday November 10th, short papers were presented followed by discussion. The subject "The depopulation of Regent and other mountain villages and how to remedy the same." The speakers were; Dr. J Abayomi-Cole, Reverend T S Johnson B.D., Reverend A E Williams L.TH., Messrs **F W Okrafor Smart** and Wilfred Cole.[61]

Francis made a plea for the provision by Government Aid, of suitable industries for the people of the villages so that they might be encouraged to stay at home developing the village resources to improve their respective villages.

Prior to the commencement of the celebrations, tributes were paid to various Regentonian families and their ancestors. Names mentioned were the Johnsons, **Smarts**, Thomasses, Farrahs, Freemans, Macauleys, Bulls, Perrys, Bucks, Randles, Coles, Congers, Thompsons, Georgestones, Metzgers, Walters, Whitfields and others.[62]

The celebrations continued with Thanksgiving Day on Sunday 10th November with a Thanksgiving Service with Holy Communion preacher Reverend R P Crabbe M.A. It ended on Monday 17th November when a group photograph was taken and at 7.00 pm a bonfire was lit on the Seven Hills surrounding Regent.

The 2nd Anniversary of Regent Centenary

The second anniversary of Regent Centenary Celebrations was observed on Sunday and Monday last, 14th and 15th November 1915.

The service in St Charles' Church, which was well decorated for the occasion, was bright and hearty. The music reflected credit on the organist Mr. M H Thompson and the choir. The licensed lay readers Messrs Samuel Macauley and James Fowler were in the procession, and took part in the services. The collections were in aid of the Church Restoration Fund. There were special female collectors in the morning with Mesdames **Mary Smart** (youngest sister of Francis), and Lucy Johnson.[63] Interesting to note Francis' sister, Mary's name involved in this service, indicating that the Smarts have established themselves as useful, good citizens of their ancestral village of Regent.

The visit to Sierra Leone of His Royal Highness The Prince of Wales.

Preparations for the arrival of the above dignitary continued for most part of 1924 for the visit in 1925.

It was proposed that the following be presented to His Royal Highness.

'Let the following be presented; not quantity but quality; men and women who have in a measure played their part in the development of the colony.' Amongst a long list of names were the following: W B Gulley, **F W Okrafor Smart** and Reaney Lampkin, all master builders.[64]

That Francis' name was put forward for this public honour of presentation to the distinguished visitor, was an indication of the high esteem with which he was held in Freetown.

Sadly in the Sierra Leone Weekly News of 8th May 1930, his death was announced.

DEATH OF MR. F W OKRAFOR SMART

It is with deep regret we have to announce the death after a few weeks illness of Mr. F W Okrafor Smart, Master Builder and Agriculturist, at 2 am on Thursday the First inst. at his residence at Bathurst Street. His remains were removed from his residence at 8.30 pm the same day, to his native village of Regent, where the burial service took place. We tender our sympathy to his widow and children, his sister Mrs. Wilfred Cole, his brothers one of whom is Dr. Smart in the Nigerian Medical Service, and other relatives. R.I.P.

11

Francis was survived by his wife Rachel Adjuah. Adjuah is a Fante name and my grandmother was born in The Gold Coast (Ghana) and was partly Ghanaian. Her father was the merchant L Cole of Freetown. My grandparents had seven children, including twin boys. Three, including the twins, died in childhood and Ayomi died aged 21 years. The remaining three were John Edowu, Draughtsman and Cartographer, Francis Balogun (my father) Draughtsman and Cartographer, Oreh William, sociologist. John Edowu married Ejuma Pratt and they produced Melissa, Leonora, Olivia and Jaydee. Unfortunately Olivia has passed away.

John Edowu Okrafo-Smart

Ejuma Okrafo-Smart

My father Francis Balogun, draughtsman and cartographer, married Sarian England (see photos). They had Victor (author), Francis, Winston, Florence, Sylvia, Ayomi, Frances and Benjamin.

Francis Okrafo-Smart, grandson of Francis John school master Isles-de-Los

Sarian Okrafo-Smart,

Oreh married Alice Butch of Chicago, U. S. A., no children, Oreh qualified as a sociologist (see photograph). He worked in Chicago, but went to Freetown, Sierra Leone, where he worked for three years and then returned to Chicago. There, he did some work with Professor Lorenzo D Turner who wrote "An Anthology of Krio Folklore and Literature" Roosevelt University, Chicago, 1963.

Oreh William Okrafo-Smart, M.Sc., (Sociology)

My father and his two brothers have all passed away, so also has my mother.

12

Conclusion

This book starts with the arrival of Okoroafor Smart First in 1816 as a Liberated African. From his lineage there came John Smart Second, the twins, my grandfather Francis, and my father Francis – five generations in all.

Okoroafor Smart First	? - 1837
John Smart Second	? - 1859?
Francis (twin brother Frederick)	1841 - 1894
Francis (grandfather)	1874 - 1930
Francis (my father)	1911 - 1970

I have been able, through archival research of original materials, to write the story of a remarkable family. If Okoroafor Smart First had not been resettled in Freetown Sierra Leone, he would have ended in the Americas, where he was destined to go in the slave ship.

Had he gone, one would never have heard anything about him, nor would I, the author, be alive today! He would have ended up as a slave to some plantation owner. He would have gone into obscurity. Without a name, a language or his African culture.

It is thanks only to the British Policy of Intervention and Resettlement in Freetown following the abolition of the slave trade in The British Empire in 1807, that made this possible.

The missionaries also played major roles in Christianising and in education, especially John Weeks who appears to have been influential in the lives of the twins Francis and Frederick. He was almost a guardian, hence the inclusion of Weeks in their family name and passed down through the generations. The missionaries sent quarterly journals to the Mission Headquarters in London. Through these journals I have been able to glean a lot of information, alongside articles and materials from Colindale Newspaper Library, London, The Heslop Library, Birmingham University, Public Records Office, London, and the Central Library, Angel Row, Nottingham.

Oral family history has also been quite useful. Especially stories told to me by my late uncle, Dr. Robert Wellesley-Cole, and my late Aunty Emma of Regent (see page 98). A special thanks must go to Mr. Christopher Fyfe, a friend of Robert. He is the expert in history of Sierra Leone about which he is the author of many books and literature. He has been inspirational to me throughout.

It has been an emotional experience for me, ranging from high emotion to deep despair, obvious expectations for one delving into family history. Throughout I have remained objective. In the end I must confess that I should count myself fortunate to have been born into a family of such talents.

Okrafo-Smart Family:
Over a Century in the Lives of a Liberated African Family

Taiwo

Photo taken at Regent on the occasion of the 80th birthday of Mrs. Taiwo Charif née Wellesley-Cole.
Picture shows some descendants of family clans; Okrafo-Smart, Wellesley-Cole and Aboko-Cole.

Okoroafor Smart First descendants continue to do well professionally. They are now spread in various parts of the world, Australia, Banjul, Canada, England, Nigeria, United States of America and, of course, Sierra Leone.

13

Some observations on the Regent Census of 1831

Photocopies of the Regent Census of 1831 from the Public Records Office (Co 267/111). It gives an interesting overview of the village with its 1766 inhabitants in a variety of occupations, three of them living in stone houses, 12 in frame houses the rest in grass huts, and many of them keeping pigs and poultry (though few have any other kind of livestock).

The returns have been made out according to a standard form used for all the Colony villages. The number of each householder, the acreage he owned, the type of house, his name, whether he was a discharged soldier (none in Regent), and his trade or general occupation. The clerks who took the census were plainly given a list of choices to fill in under occupation, as "farmer", "trader" etc. One of them was "agriculturalist" but what was supposed to distinguish this occupation from "farmer"? As you will see, the clerk who made out the Regent census spelt it "agriculturies". Then follow details of family (unfortunately the way the volume had to be photocopied, without breaking has made some of these illegible). Number of Liberated African Apprentices, then a heading rendered by the Clerk "Newly Emancipated Africans living with the inhabitants until their domestics are finished" (i.e. until they are domesticated into the new ways of life in the colony). Natives of the country adjacent to the colony living with the inhabitants of the District (none in Regent), Liberated African children who are too young to be apprenticed and placed at school, the totals, stock and remarks. My ancestor John Smart is identified in census as number 447.

Europeans were not included in the census. The census forms, which were bound up in one volume (CO 267/111), were sent to the Colonial Office by Governor Findlay with a covering despatch, which includes a report on the villages (CO 267/109). Findlay No 16 7th May 1831 with an enthusiastic account of Regent and of Weeks' work there[65].

Okrafo-Smart Family: Over a Century in the Lives of a Liberated African Family

Village or Hamlet	Allotment (Town/Country)		House			Name of Proprietor		Trade or General Occupation
	Town	Country	Stone	Frame	Clay	Lib'd African	Disch'd Soldier	
Regent Town	1	..	..	..	1	Thomas Farah		Farmer
	2	..	..	..	1	Thomas Flood		Trader
	3	2	..	..	1	Jim Thompson		Shinglemaker
	4	..	..	..	1	Jim Chamber		Labour
	5	3	..	..	1	Enaboo		Farmer
	6	..	1	..	..	David Noah		Writer
	7	3	..	..	1	Luke Mudday		Sawyer
	8	3	..	1	..	John Catte Catty		Farmer
	9	1	..	..	1	Joe Mill		Sailor
	10	2	..	..	1	Arboocks		Farmer
	11	3	..	..	1	John Farmer		do
	12	2	..	..	1	Manquah		Labour
	13	1	..	..	1	Billey Bull		Shinglemaker
	14	2	..	..	1	John Farmer		Farmer
	15	2	1	..	..	Peter Hughes		Mason
	16	..	..	..	1	Isaac Bull		Labour
	17	4	..	..	1	Joseph During		Farmer
	18	1	..	..	1	Thomas Hughes		Labour
	19	..	..	..	1	Peter Green		Mason
	20	1	..	..	1	John Gandon		Labour
	21	..	..	..	1	Doctor Paul		do
	22	2	..	..	1	John Arbassah		do
	23	1	..	..	1	Toyaccom		do
	24	3	..	..	1	John Peter		do
	25	..	..	..	1	John Hartebit		do
	26	1	..	..	1	Ceman		do
	27	2	..	..	1	Affoo		do
		39	2	1	24	27	-	2

Okrafo-Smart Family: Over a Century in the Lives of a Liberated African Family

Village or Hamlet	Town or Country allotment		House			Name of Proprietor		Trade or General Occupation
	Town	Country No of acres	Stone	Frame	Crnel	Lib.d African	Disch.d Soldier	
	"	39	2	1	24	27	"	
	28	1	"	"	1	Jim Mammah		Labour
	29	1	"	"	1	Thomas Green		Mas.
	30	1	"	"	1	John Crowbah		Mas.
	31	3	"	"	1	Thomas Ishi.		Labour
	32	"	"	"	1	Mary Davis		Do
	33	"	"	"	1	Ocorrequah		Do
	34	1	"	"	1	Jim Peter		Do
	35	3	"	"	1	Tom Macaulay		Do
	36	1	"	"	1	Joe Fever		Do
	37	3	"	"	1	Sam Peter		Farmer
	38	1	"	"	1	William Jack		Labour
	39	2	"	"	1	Ocorros		Do
	40	2	"	"	1	Sam John		Do
	41	"	"	"	1	Jim Callabah		Do
	42	1	"	"	1	John Macaulay		Do
	43	2	"	"	1	Jim Kargah		Do
	44	"	"	"	1	Henry George		Do
	45	1	"	"	1	Joe Dick		Do
	46	"	"	"	1	Peter John		Do
	47	1	"	"	1	Sam Pratt		Do
	48	"	"	"	1	Joe Cnuckkos		Do
	49	"	"	"	1	Sam Squaragay		Do
	50	1	"	"	1	Will		Do
	51	1	"	"	1	Sam Grant 1st		Do
	52	1	"	"	1	Sam Grant 2d		Do
	53	2	"	"	1	Sally Hughes		Do
	54	1	"	"	1	Sam Fever		Do
	55	1	"	"	1	Jim Cole		Do
		70	2	1	52	55		

52

Persons Occupied: Family, Wife	Children, Male	Children, Female	Liberated African Apprentices, Male	Liberated African Apprentices, Female	Newly emancipated Africans living with the inhabitants as their domestics or servants, Male	Newly emancipated Africans..., Female	Natives of the country adjacent to the Colony living with the inhabitants of the District, Male	Natives of the country..., Female	Liberated African children who are too young to be apprenticed and placed at school, Male	Liberated African children..., Female	Total Population, Male	Total Population, Female	Stock: Horses	Asses	Cows	Oxen	Sheep	Goats	Pigs	Heads of Poultry	Remarks
20	18	13	15	2	5	1	-	-	-	-	65	36	-	-	1	-	-	-	15	44	
-	-	-	-	-	-	-	-	-	-	-	1	-	-	-	-	-	-	-	-	-	
-	-	1	-	-	-	-	-	-	-	-	1	1	-	-	-	-	-	-	-	-	
1	-	1	-	-	-	-	-	-	-	-	1	2	-	-	-	-	-	-	-	-	
1	1	1	1	1	-	-	-	-	-	-	3	3	-	-	1	-	2	-	-	6	
-	-	-	-	-	-	-	-	-	-	-	1	-	-	-	-	-	-	-	-	-	
1	1	2	-	-	-	-	-	-	-	-	2	3	-	-	-	-	-	-	-	-	an Invalid
1	-	-	1	-	-	-	-	-	-	-	2	1	-	-	-	-	-	-	-	-	
1	-	-	-	-	1	-	-	-	-	-	2	1	-	-	-	-	-	-	1	-	
1	-	-	-	-	-	-	-	-	-	-	1	1	-	-	-	-	-	-	-	-	
1	-	-	-	-	1	-	-	-	-	-	2	1	-	-	-	-	-	-	1	-	
1	-	-	-	-	-	-	-	-	-	-	1	1	-	-	-	-	-	-	-	4	
1	-	1	-	-	1	-	-	-	-	-	2	2	-	-	-	-	-	-	1	4	
1	2	3	1	-	1	-	-	-	-	-	5	4	-	-	-	-	-	-	1	-	
1	1	1	-	-	-	-	-	-	-	-	2	2	-	-	-	-	-	-	-	-	an Invalid
1	1	-	-	-	-	-	-	-	-	-	2	1	-	-	-	-	-	-	-	-	
1	1	-	-	1	1	-	-	-	-	-	3	2	-	-	-	-	-	-	1	-	
1	1	-	-	-	-	-	-	-	-	-	2	1	-	-	-	-	-	-	-	-	an Invalid
1	-	-	-	-	-	-	-	-	-	-	1	1	-	-	-	-	-	-	-	-	
1	-	-	-	-	-	-	-	-	-	-	1	1	-	-	-	-	-	-	-	3	
1	-	1	1	-	-	-	-	-	-	-	2	2	-	-	-	-	-	-	1	-	
1	-	-	-	-	-	-	-	-	-	-	1	1	-	-	-	-	-	-	1	-	
1	-	2	-	-	-	-	-	-	-	-	1	3	-	-	-	-	-	-	1	2	
1	-	-	-	-	-	-	-	-	-	-	1	-	-	-	-	-	-	-	-	-	
1	1	2	-	-	-	-	-	-	-	-	2	3	-	-	-	-	-	-	1	-	
1	-	-	-	-	-	-	-	-	-	-	1	1	-	-	-	-	-	-	1	-	
-	-	1	-	-	-	-	-	-	-	-	1	1	-	-	-	-	-	-	1	3	
1	1	-	-	-	-	-	-	-	-	-	2	1	-	-	-	-	-	-	2	3	
1	2	1	-	-	-	-	-	-	-	-	3	2	-	-	-	-	-	-	1	3	
44	30	30	19	4	10	-	-	-	-	-	114	78	-	-	2	-	2	-	39	72	

Okrafo-Smart Family:
Over a Century in the Lives of a Liberated African Family

Village or Hamlet	Town or Country allotment		House			Name of Proprietor Liberated African	By how many persons Discharged Soldier	Trade or General Occupation
		70	2	1	52	55		
	56	1	"	"	1	Peter Paul		Tavern
	57	1	"	"	1	Jim Juke		Do
	58	2	"	1	"	Peter Smart		Do
	59	2	"	"	1	Sam Juke		Do
	60	1	"	"	1	William Macauley		Do
	61	1	"	"	1	Dick Raffell		Do
	62	1	"	"	1	Sam John		Do
	63	1	"	"	1	Joe Oliver		Do
	64	1	"	"	1	George William		Do
	65	2	"	"	1	Jim George		Do
	66	2	"	"	1	Thomas William		Do
	67	1	"	"	1	Commodore		Sawyer
	68	3	"	"	1	Peter John		Do
	69	"	"	"	1	Eworrah		Sawyer
	70	1	"	"	1	William Davis		Farmer
	71	1	"	"	1	Worros		Do
	72	2	"	"	1	Tom Okoro		Do
	73	1	"	"	1	John Jim		Do
	74	2	"	"	1	Arlauromah		Do
	75	2	"	"	1	Jim Prate		Do
	76	2	"	"	1	William Labour		Do
	77	"	"	"	1	Leopold Judas		Do
	78	1	"	"	1	David		
	79	2	"	"	1	Sam Davis		Shinglemaker
	80	1	"	"	1	Sam Johnson		Labour
	81	1	"	"	1	Ockoo		Do
	82	"	"	"	1	Sabboh		Do
	83	1	"	"	1	Peter Davis		Farmer
	"	106	2	2	79	83		

Regent continued

53

...ccupied								Liberated African Children who are too young to be ... and placed at school		Total Population		Stock								Remarks
...mily Children		Liberated African Apprentices		Newly emancipated Africans living with the inhabitants until their masters are found		Natives of the Country ...						Horses	Asses	Cows	Oxen	Sheep	Goat	Pigs	Heads of ...	
Male	Female	Male	Female	Male	Female	Male	Female	Male	Female	Male	Female									
30	30	19	4	10	-	-	-	-	-	114	78	-	-	2	-	2	-	29	72	
1	-	-	-	-	-	-	-	-	-	2	1	-	-	-	-	-	-	-	-	
-	1	1	-	-	-	-	-	-	-	2	2	-	-	-	-	-	-	-	-	
-	-	1	-	-	-	-	-	-	-	2	1	-	-	-	-	-	-	-	2	
-	-	-	-	-	-	-	-	-	-	1	1	-	-	-	-	-	-	1	4	
-	1	-	-	-	-	-	-	-	-	1	2	-	-	-	-	-	-	2	5	
-	-	-	-	-	-	-	-	-	-	1	1	-	-	-	-	-	-	1	2	
-	-	-	-	-	-	-	-	-	-	1	1	-	-	-	-	-	-	2	2	
2	-	-	-	-	-	-	-	-	-	3	1	-	-	-	-	-	-	1	-	
-	1	-	-	-	-	-	-	-	-	1	2	-	-	-	-	-	-	-	-	
-	-	-	-	-	-	-	-	-	-	1	1	-	-	-	-	-	-	2	7	
-	-	-	-	1	-	-	-	-	-	2	-	-	-	-	-	-	-	-	-	
-	-	-	-	-	-	-	-	-	-	1	-	-	-	-	-	-	-	-	-	
-	1	-	-	-	-	-	-	-	-	1	2	-	-	-	-	-	-	-	2	
1	2	-	-	-	-	-	-	-	-	2	3	-	-	-	-	-	-	-	-	
1	-	-	-	-	-	-	-	-	-	2	1	-	-	-	-	-	-	-	-	
-	1	-	-	-	-	-	-	-	-	1	1	-	-	-	-	-	-	-	-	
-	-	-	-	-	-	-	-	-	-	1	-	-	-	-	-	-	-	-	-	
-	1	-	-	-	-	-	-	-	-	1	2	-	-	-	-	-	-	1	-	
-	-	-	-	-	-	-	-	-	-	1	-	-	-	-	-	-	-	-	-	
-	-	-	-	-	-	-	-	-	-	1	1	-	-	-	-	-	-	1	3	
1	2	-	-	-	-	-	-	-	-	2	3	-	-	-	-	5	-	2	4	
1	1	1	-	-	-	-	-	-	-	3	1	-	-	-	-	-	-	-	2	
3	1	-	-	-	-	-	-	-	-	4	2	-	-	-	-	-	-	-	-	
-	-	-	-	-	-	-	-	-	-	1	1	-	-	-	-	-	-	-	-	
-	-	-	-	-	-	-	-	-	-	1	1	-	-	-	-	-	-	-	-	
-	-	-	-	-	-	-	-	-	-	1	1	-	-	-	-	-	-	-	-	
1	-	-	-	-	-	-	-	-	-	2	1	-	-	-	-	-	-	-	-	
-	1	-	-	-	-	-	-	-	-	1	2	-	-	-	-	-	-	-	-	
41	43	22	4	11	-	-	-	-	-	157	113	-	-	2	-	7	-	42	105	

Okrafo-Smart Family:
Over a Century in the Lives of a Liberated African Family

Village or Hamlet	Town or Country allotment		House			Name of Proprietor		Trade or General Occupation
	Town	Country	Stone	Frame	Clay	Lib[d] African	Disc[d] Soldier	
	-	106	2	2	79	83	-	
	84	2	"	"	1	Sam		Labour
	85	3	"	"	1	William Kargah		Farmer
	86	2	"	"	1	Peter Flood 1st		Agricultr[l]
	87	2	"	"	1	Sam Allen		Do
	88	2	"	"	1	John Johnson		Do
	89	2	"	1	"	Sam John		Do
	90	2	"	"	1	Tom Hughes		Do
	91	2	"	"	1	Peter Flood 2d		Do
	92	3	"	"	1	John Smart		Do
	93	2	"	"	1	John Bull		Do
	94	2	"	"	1	John Decker		Do
	95	1	"	"	1	Jim John		Do
	96	2	"	"	1	William Walter		Tailor
	97	2	"	"	1	George House		Labour
	98	2	"	"	1	John Taylor		Do
	99	"	"	"	1	Thomas Johnson		Do
	100	2	"	"	1	Thomas Decker		Mason
	101	2	"	"	1	Ajah		Farmer
	102	1	"	"	1	John William		Do
	103	2	"	"	1	Joe Cook		Do
	104	1	"	"	1	Samuel		Do
	105	2	"	"	1	Joe		Labour
	106	1	"	"	1	Jim Nick		Do
	107	"	"	"	1	Robert Pierce		Do
	108	1	"	"	1	Jim Foulah		Do
	109	2	"	"	1	William Decker		Do
	110	2	"	"	1	George Ebazim		Farmer
	111	1	"	"	1	John Chamber		Shinglemaker
		155	2	3	106	111	-	

Report continued

Okrafo-Smart Family: Over a Century in the Lives of a Liberated African Family

Okrafo-Smart Family:
Over a Century in the Lives of a Liberated African Family

Village or hamlet	Town or country allotment		House		Name of Proprietor	By how many	Trade or General Occupation
					Lib.d African	Disch.d Soldier	
	" 155	2	3	106	111	—	
	112	1	"	"	1 Phillip		Sawyer
	113	1	"	"	1 Allarmah		Do
	114	2	"	"	1 Marlarbarlee		Labo.r
	115	1	"	"	1 Ahsemannah		Sawyer
	116	"	"	"	1 Matildia		
Regent continued	117	3	"	"	1 John Doctor		Labour
	118	3	"	"	1 Peter Bull		Shingleman
	119	2	"	"	1 John		Labour
	120	1	"	"	1 Henry McCarthy		Sailor
	121	1	"	1	" Abraham Farrah		Batschr
	122	"	"	"	1 John Isaac Johnson		Shingleman
	123	"	"	"	1 Isaac Morgan		Mason
	124	2	"	"	1 Pearce		Agricult.
	125	1	"	"	1 Joseph Chamber		Shingleman
	126	2	"	"	1 Thomas Sawyer		Sawyer
	127	2	"	"	1 Will		Labour
	128	2	"	"	1 Jim		Do
	129	2	"	"	1 George Kakebah		Do
	130	"	"	"	1 John Peter		Do
	131	1	"	"	1 John Morgan		Do
	132	2	"	"	1 Sombo Inquah		Do
	133	1	"	"	1 Tom Davis		Sawyr.
	134	2	"	"	1 Tom McCarthy		Farmer
	135	2	"	"	1 John William		Do
	136	"	"	"	1 Sam Paul		Shingleman
	137	2	"	"	1 Tom Bulle Cutty		Sawyer
	158	1	"	"	1 George Davis		Labour
	192	2	4	132	138	—	

Okrafo-Smart Family: Over a Century in the Lives of a Liberated African Family

Village or hamlet	Town or Country allotment No. of Acres	House Stone	House Frame	Name of Proprietor Lib.d African	Disc.d Soldier	By how many Trade or Means Pension
	192	2	4	132	138	—
	139 1	"	"	1 Jim Thompson		Labour
	140 2	"	"	1 J York		Do
	141 2	"	"	1 C gay		Do
	142 1	"	"	1 William		Labour
	143 "	"	"	1 Sam During		Farmer
	144 "	"	"	1 John Gamsay		Do
	145 2	"	"	1 John Barber		Do
	146 1	"	"	1 Arkebejah		Labour
	147 "	"	"	1 Eyeajoe		Boatman
Ryent continued	148 2	"	"	1 Ochoh		Labour
	149 2	"	"	1 Thomas Lottafoo		Agricult
	150 2	"	"	1 Obassah		Do
	151 2	"	"	1 Jim Croah		Do
	152 2	"	"	1 John Morgan		Do
	153 1	"	"	1 Ire Dick		Do
	154 2	"	"	1 Day linoo		Do
	155 2	"	"	1 Arbojaeroo		Do
	156 1	"	"	1 Asseepah		Do
	157 2	"	"	1 Arbombs		Do
	158 2	"	"	1 Ochoh		Do
	159 2	"	"	1 Ogha		Do
	160 1	"	"	1 Jebbodoo		Do
	161 1	"	"	1 Sarsoorah		Do
	162 1	"	"	1 Lookoo		Labour
	163 1	"	"	1 Koojah		Do
	164 1	"	"	1 John Davis		Do
	165 "	"	"	1 Dick Snow		Labour
	166 1	"	"	1 Sayesoo		Do
	229	2	4	160	166	—

Okrafo-Smart Family: Over a Century in the Lives of a Liberated African Family

Village or Hamlet	Town or Country allotment		House			Name of Proprietor		
	Town No.	Country No. of Acres	Stone	Frame	Wood	Liberated Africans	Disch Soldier	
		329	2	4	160	166	—	
	167	1	"	"	1	Aggidong		Lab
	168	1	"	"	1	John Davis		Lab
	169	1	"	"	1	William Gainor		Far
	170	1	"	"	1	Thomas Robinson		Lab
	171	1	"	"	1	John Calvin		Fach
	172	1	"	"	1	Thomas Howard		Coop
	173	"	"	"	1	Joe Yamsay		Saw
	174	2	"	"	1	Jessah		Lab
Regent continued	175	1	"	"	"	John Smith		Do
	176	3	"	"	1	John Yprofe		Do
	177	2	"	"	1	Abraham Johnson		Shing
	178	1	"	"	1	William Bucknor		Lab
	179	2	"	"	1	Peter Thomas		Do
	180	"	"	"	1	William Johnson		Do
	181	"	"	"	1	Arcarrah		Saw
	182	1	"	"	1	Affankaray		Do
	183	1	"	"	1	Jim Kendall		Do
	184	1	"	"	1	Harry Joe		Lab
	185	1	"	"	1	John Mackey		Do
	186	1	"	"	1	Saggoon		Do
	187	1	"	"	1	Chowoo		Do
	188	1	"	"	1	Tom		Do
	189	"	"	"	1	Owan		Do
	190	5	"	"	1	Josiah Yamsay		Baily
	191	1	"	"	1	John Davis		Boatm
	192	1	"	"	1	Defond		Lab
	193	1	"	"	1	John Taylor		Shingl
	194	2	"	"	1	Benjamin Johnson		Farm
	195	2	"	"	1	William George		Sawy
		265	2	4	109	195	—	

Okrafo-Smart Family: Over a Century in the Lives of a Liberated African Family

Village or Hamlet	No.	No. of acres	Slave	Finance	[House]	Name of Proprietor	Lib'd African / [Brick] / Soldier	[Occupation]
Regent continued		365	2	4	189	195	—	
	196	2	"	"	1	Joe Grant		Sawyer
	197	2	"	"	1	James Whip		Mason
	198	2	"	"	1	Samuel Parker		Carpenter
	199	1	"	"	1	John Lever		Farmer
	200	1	"	"	1	Harry Johnson		Shoemaker
	201	2	"	"	1	John Cumorcom		Farmer
	202	2	"	"	1	James Hughes		Mason
	203	1	"	"	1	Thomas Rendall		Carpenter
	204	1	"	"	1	Sam Johnson		Labourer
	205	1	"	"	1	William Johnson		Mason
	206	1	"	"	1	Appiah		Agricult.
	207	1	"	"	1	Thomas Decker		Mason
	208	1	"	"	1	Sam Smith		Farmer
	209	1	"	"	1	John Free		Do
	210	1	"	"	1	Joseph Johnson		Mason
	211	2	"	"	1	Sam Lever		Labourer
	212	2	"	"	1	James Wran		Do
	213	1	"	"	1	Dinghorn Smith		Do
	214	"	"	"	—	Indecker		Do
	215	1	"	"	1	Ayso		Do
	216	1	"	"	1	Imbang Ire		Do
	217	1	"	"	1	John Quarber		Do
	218	5	"	1	—	Peter Combert		Carpenter
	219	3	"	"	1	Thomas Bull		Farmer
	220	"	"	"	1	Jim Bull		Labourer
	221	1	"	"	1	Henry leDecker		Mason
	222	1	"	"	1	Harry Sutherland		Carpenter
	223	"	"	"	1	Mary Ballah		Agricult.
	224	2	"	"	1	John Sharp		Do
	225	1	"	"	1	Jim Ire		Do
		309	2	5	217	225	—	

Okrafo-Smart Family: Over a Century in the Lives of a Liberated African Family

Okrafo-Smart Family:
Over a Century in the Lives of a Liberated African Family

Village or Hamlet	Town or Country allotment Town	Country	Houses New	Framed	Filled	Name of Proprietor	Lib. Africans	Disch. Soldier	Trade or General occupation
		309	2	5	217	225		—	
	226	2	.	.	1	William Macaulay			Farmer
	227	2	.	.	1	George William			do
	228	1	.	.	1	Henry Bull			do
	229	1	.	.	1	Joe Buring			do
	230	1	.	.	1	Sam			do
	231	1	.	.	1	Tim Collin			do
	232	2	.	.	1	Peter Shaw			do
	233	1	.	.	1	Harry Macaulay			do
Regent continued	234	1	.	.	1	Jim Johnson			Constable
	235	.	.	.	.	Peter Sawyer			do
	236	1	.	.	1	Mary William			do
	237	1	.	.	1	Joe Thomas			do
	238	2	.	.	1	Thomas Pesty			Carpenter
	239	1	.	.	1	Henry Davis			Labour
	240	1	.	.	1	Sam Davis			do
	241	.	.	.	.	Aquallay			do
	242	1	1	.	1	John Taylor			do
	243	1	.	.	1	Peter Walker			do
	244	.	.	.	1	Joe Sou Hound			do
	245	1	.	.	1	Owanbill			do
	246	.	.	.	1	Sam Young			do
	247	.	.	.	1	Qesam			do
	248	2	.	.	1	Sam John			Sailor
	249	1	.	.	1	John Baker			Labour
	250	3	.	.	1	Robert Bickustt			Sailor
	251	2	.	.	1	John Doggo			Shoemaker
		338	2	5	242	251		—	

Liberated Africans Apprenticed	newly emancipated Africans living with the Inhabitants Domestics &c repaired	natives of the country &c accept with colony living with the Inhabitants of the District	Liberated African Children who are too young to be Apprenticed one placed at School		Total Population		Stock							Remarks
males	females	males	females	males	females	males	females	males	females	Horses	Mules	Cows	Oxen	Pigs	Goats	Sheep Poultry	
99	44	19	15	4	"	"	"	"	368	304	"	15	"	9	9	16	348	
"	"	"	"	"	"	"	"	a	1	1	"	"	"	"	"	"	"	
"	"	2	"	"	"	"	"	"	2	1	"	"	"	"	"	"	"	
"	"	"	"	"	"	"	"	"	3	1	"	"	"	"	"	"	2	
"	11	"	"	"	"	"	"	"	1	1	"	"	"	"	"	"	2	
1	"	"	"	"	"	"	"	"	1	2	"	"	"	"	"	"	2	
"	"	"	"	"	"	"	"	"	2	1	"	"	"	"	"	"	"	
"	"	"	"	"	"	"	"	"	2	1	"	"	"	"	"	"	3	
2	1	1	"	"	"	"	"	"	2	4	"	"	"	2	1	"	3	
"	2	2	"	"	"	"	"	"	4	3	"	"	"	3	4	"	10	
"	"	"	"	"	"	"	"	"	1	1	"	"	"	"	"	"	"	
"	1	"	"	"	"	"	"	"	3	1	"	"	"	"	"	"	"	
1	"	"	"	"	"	"	"	"	1	"	"	"	"	"	"	"	"	
1	"	"	"	"	"	"	"	"	3	2	"	"	"	"	"	"	"	
"	"	"	"	"	"	"	"	"	1	1	"	"	"	"	"	"	"	
"	1	"	"	"	"	"	"	"	2	1	"	"	"	"	"	"	3	
2	"	"	"	"	"	"	"	"	"	3	"	"	"	"	"	"	"	
2	"	"	"	"	"	"	"	"	"	3	"	"	"	"	"	1	6	
"	"	"	"	"	"	"	"	"	1	"	"	"	"	"	"	"	"	
"	"	"	"	"	"	"	"	"	2	"	"	"	"	"	"	"	"	
"	"	"	"	"	"	"	"	"	1	"	"	"	"	"	"	"	"	
1	"	"	"	"	"	"	"	"	"	2	"	"	"	"	"	"	"	
1	"	"	"	"	"	"	"	"	1	2	"	"	"	"	"	"	3	
"	"	"	"	"	"	"	"	"	"	2	"	"	"	"	"	"	2	
"	"	"	"	"	"	"	"	"	2	1	"	"	"	"	"	"	3	
"	"	"	"	"	"	"	"	"	1	"	"	"	"	"	"	"	2	
111	48	22	15	4	"	"	"	"	410	339	"	15	"	20	14	18	387	

Okrafo-Smart Family:
Over a Century in the Lives of a Liberated African Family

Village or Hamlet	Town or country (Farm / Country / crop / Acres)		House (Stone / Frame / ?)			Name of Proprietor (Lib.d African / Disb.d Soldier)		By how many Pers.d (Trade or General Occupation)
		338	2	5	242	257		
	252	2	„	„	1	Ingalloo		Labourer
	253	2	„	„	1	Isaak Norman		Do
	254	1	„	„	1	Cutkate		Do
	255	„	„	„	1	William Johnson		Do
	256	1	„	„	1	Joseph During		Shoemaker
	257	.	„	„	1	William Hyde		Labour
	258	2	„	„	1	John Tho.s Johnson		Mason
	259	2	„	„	1	Dick Macarthy		Farmer
	260	2	„	„	1	Dorrey		Sawyer
	261	2	„	„	1	Cato		Do
	262	1	„	„	1	Daniel Green		Farmer
Regent continued	263	1	1	„	„	Sack Nicol +		Sawyer
	264	1	„	„	1	Tom.e Macaulay		Do
	265	1	„	„	1	Sam Parkinson		Do
	266	1	„	„	1	Tom Haseley		Shinglemaker
	267	1	„	„	1	William Morgan		Carpenter
	268	1	„	„	1	William MacMillan		Shinglemaker
	269	1	„	„	1	Mackal		Sawyer
	270	1	„	„	1	Tom Weakfall		Do
	271	2	„	„	1	Sam Smith		Bl.Smith
	272	2	„	„	1	William Toulah		Farmer
	273	1	„	„	1	Water Carrier		Do
	274	2	„	„	1	Sam Davis		Do
	275	2	„	„	1	John Johnson		Mason
	276	2	„	„	1	Thomas Thompson		Farmer
	277	2	„	„	1	Thomas Norman		Carpenter
	278	3	„	„	1	Thomas Macaulay		Farmer
		377	3	5	268	278	. . „	

Okrafo-Smart Family: Over a Century in the Lives of a Liberated African Family

Village or Hamlet	Town or Country allotment No.	No. of acres	House New	House Frame	House Crust	Name of Proprietor (Liberated African)	Disch'd Soldier	Trade or General occupation
	"	377	3	5	268	278	"	
	279	2	"	"	1	Paulos		Farmer
	280	2	"	"	1	Peter Gamsday		Do
	281	2	"	"	1	John William		Do
	282	3	"	"	1	William Taylor		Do
	283	1	"	1	"	John Johnson		Do
	284	3	"	"	1	Thomas Doctor		Agriculture
	285	2	"	"	1	Inquatoo		Labour
	286	3	"	"	1	Sam Macaulay		Do
Regent returned	287	2	"	"	1	Tom Lamp		Do
	288	2	"	"	1	Peter Green		Mason
	289	1	"	"	1	Solomon Duanquim		Farmer
	290	1	"	"	1	Kanawah		Do
	291	2	"	"	1	Bee Macaulay		Do
	292	1	"	"	1	Come		Do
	293	2	"	"	1	Ingancocoa		Do
	294	2	"	"	1	John Peter		Do
	295	2	"	"	1	Joseph Pratt		Mason
	296	2	"	"	1	Geo Macaulay		Mason
	297	2	"	"	1	Abraham Davis		Shinglemaker
	298	"	"	"	1	William Sharp		Labour
	299	2	"	"	1	Thomas Decker		Farmer
	300	1	"	"	1	Tim Dickson		Do
	301	2	"	"	1	William Decker		Do
	302	1	"	"	1	William Dickson		Labour
	303	1	"	"	1	Sumookong		Do
	304	1	"	"	1	Thomas Corem		Do
		410	3	6	293	304	"	

Okrafo-Smart Family: Over a Century in the Lives of a Liberated African Family

Persons Occupied								Total Population		Stock							
Liberated Africans		Newly arrived Liberated Africans living with the inhabitants until their Domestic arrangements are finished		Natives of the country adjacent to the Colony living with the inhabitants		Liberated African children who are now young to be apprenticed and placed at school				Horses	Asses	Cows	Oxen	Sheep	Goats	Pigs	Head of Poultry	Remarks
Males	Females	Males	Females	Males	Females	Males	Females	Males	Females								
130	56	25	17	7	"	"	"	465	388	"	"	13	"	22	10	86	416
"	"	"	"	"	"	"	"	1	1	"	"	"	"	"	"	2	"
"	"	"	"	"	"	"	"	1	1	"	"	"	"	"	"	"	"
"	"	"	"	"	"	"	"	1	1	"	"	"	"	"	"	3	3
"	1	"	"	2	"	"	"	2	3	"	"	"	"	"	9	2	2
1	"	"	"	"	"	"	"	1	2	1	"	"	"	"	"	4	2
1	1	"	"	"	"	"	"	3	2	"	"	"	"	"	"	2	4
"	"	"	"	"	"	"	"	1	2	"	"	"	"	"	"	1	"
"	"	"	"	"	"	"	"	1	1	"	"	"	"	"	"	"	"
"	"	"	"	"	"	"	"	"	2	"	"	"	"	"	"	"	"
2	1	"	"	1	"	"	"	2	4	"	"	"	"	"	"	5	"
1	"	1	"	"	"	"	"	3	3	"	"	"	"	"	"	"	6
"	"	"	"	"	"	"	"	1	1	"	"	"	"	"	"	3	3
1	1	"	"	"	"	"	"	3	2	"	"	"	"	"	"	"	"
"	"	"	"	"	"	"	"	1	"	"	"	"	"	"	"	"	"
"	1	"	"	"	"	"	"	2	2	"	"	"	"	"	"	3	3
1	"	"	"	"	"	"	"	"	2	"	"	"	"	"	"	"	"
"	"	"	"	"	"	"	"	"	1	"	"	"	"	"	"	"	4
1	"	"	"	"	"	"	"	"	2	"	"	"	"	"	"	"	4
2	"	"	"	"	"	"	"	2	3	"	"	"	"	"	"	1	"
"	"	"	"	"	"	"	"	"	"	"	"	"	"	"	"	"	"
"	3	"	"	"	"	"	"	"	"	"	"	"	"	"	"	2	2
"	"	"	"	"	"	"	"	5	1	"	"	"	"	"	"	2	2
2	1	"	"	"	"	"	"	4	3	"	"	1	"	"	"	1	7
"	"	"	"	"	"	"	"	1	1	"	"	"	"	"	"	"	6
"	"	"	"	"	"	"	"	"	1	"	"	"	"	"	"	"	"
1	"	"	"	"	"	"	"	1	2	"	"	"	"	"	"	"	"
145	64	26	17	10	"	"	"	512	430	"	"	16	"	20	19	"	456

Village or hamlet	Town or Country allotments		House			Names of Proprietor			Trade or General Occupation
	Town No of acres	Country	Stone	Frame	Ord.	Lib.d African	Disp.d	Soldier	
	·	410	3	6	293	304			
	305	1	"	"	1	William Davis			Labour
	306	2	"	"	1	Sudoh			Do
	307	1	"	"	1	Manawar			Do
	308	2	"	"	1	Sue Daring			Mason
	309	2	"	"	1	Moses Walker			Agriculture
	310	·	"	"	1	Incombah			Do
	311	1	"	"	1	John Thorpe			Do
	312	3	"	"	1	Tom Fewr			Do
	313	2	"	"	1	Tom William			Do
	314	2	"	"	1	Coombah			Do
	315	2	"	"	1	Nancy Wankongo			
Regent continued	316	2	"	"	1	Peter Kiffele			Agriculture
	317	1	"	"	1	Alembah			Do
	318	1	"	"	1	Stoomackah			Do
	319	2	"	"	1	Thomas Mongo			Labour
	320	2	"	"	1	Sarah William			
	321	2	"	"	1	Pynloo P			Labour
	322	2	"	"	1	Gunpair			Do
	323	1	"	"	1	Gamsay			Shinglemaker
	324	2	"	"	1	Jack Smart			Labour
	325	1	"	"	1	Aulobennah			Sailor
	326	2	"	"	1	Jacob Macauly			Labour
	327	2	"	"	1	Thomas Mongo			Do
	328	2	"	"	1	William Macauly			Do
	329	2	"	"	1	Thomas Morgan			Do
	330	1	"	"	1	Aulobaullobannah			Do
	331	2	"	"	1	William Daring			Do
	332	2	"	"	1	John Wm River			Sawyer
	333	1	"	"	1	Peter Grant			Labour
	334	2	"	"	1	John Norman			Do
	335	1	"	"	1	Peter Banyan			Do
		460	3	6	324	335			

Okrafo-Smart Family: Over a Century in the Lives of a Liberated African Family

Okrafo-Smart Family: Over a Century in the Lives of a Liberated African Family

Village or Hamlet	Town or Country allotment (Town lot or acres) / (Country)	House (Stone) (Frame) (Wattle)			Name of Proprietor (Liberated African)	Disch'd Soldier	Trade or General Occupation	
		460	3	6	324	335	—	275
	336	1	"	"	1	Bannah		Labour
	337	"	"	"	1	Sandro		do
	338	2	"	"	1	Thomas Johnson		Farmer
	339	2	"	"	1	Jim Pendah		do
	340	1	"	"	1	William Riffell		Sawyer
	341	1	"	"	1	James Cates		Farmer
	342	2	"	"	1	Thomas Wanton		Tailor
	343	3	"	"	1	John Smith		Farmer
	344	2	"	"	1	Sam Macaulay		do
	345	2	"	"	1	Joseph Riffell		do
	346	1	"	"	1	William Macaulay		Labour
Regent continued	347	2	"	"	1	Bangcoombah		Farmer
	348	"	"	"	1	Hallie Macaulay		
	349	2	"	"	1	Thomas Bull		Labour
	350	1	"	"	1	Lockenrockperrah		do
	351	2	"	"	1	Jim Morrison		do
	352	1	"	"	1	John Macaulay		Tailor
	353	1	"	"	1	Betsy Johnson		
	354	2	"	"	1	Thomas Horton		Tailor
	355	1	"	"	1	William Chamber		Shinglemaker
	356	2	"	"	1	Josiah Pratt		Tailor
	357	1	"	"	1	George Johnson		Mason
	358	3	"	"	1	Harry Bell		Mason
	359	2	"	"	1	Charles Cole		Farmer
	360	"	"	"	1	William Peter		Mason
	361	1	"	"	1	Benrambah		Farmer
	362	"	"	1	"	Thomas Bridey		Carpenter
	363	1	"	"	1	John Decker		Mason
	364	2	"	"	1	John Wm Johnson		Labour
	365	2	"	"	1	Jim Nick		Mason
	366	1	"	"	1	William Herbert		Carpenter
		504	3	7	353	366	—	29

Village or Hamlet	Town or Country allotment		House		Name of Proprietor		Trade or General Occupation	
	Town	Country	Stone	Frame	Lib.d African	Disch.d Soldier		
	504	3	7	353	366	—		
	367	2	"	1	1 John Wm Johnson		Constable	
	368	2	"	"	1 William During		Mason	
	369	1	"	"	1 Jackson		Sawyer	
	370	1	"	"	1 James McCarthy		Labour	
	371	2	"	"	1 Thomas Pender		Do	
	372	2	"	"	1 Jim Momodoo		Mason	
	373	1	"	"	1 Combolli		Labour	
	374	2	"	"	1 John Smith		Farmer	
	375	2	"	"	1 John Davis		Labour	
	376	1	"	"	1 John Raffell		Do	
	377	1	"	"	1 Peter Samsay		Do	
	378	1	"	"	1 Barrah		Do	
	379	1	"	"	1 Thomas Taylor		Carpenter	
	380	2	"	1	" William Weston		Carpenter	
	381	2	"	1	" Peter Green		Mason	
	382	2	"	"	1 Thomas Paulo		Mason	
	383	1	"	"	1 James Square		Labour	
	384	1	"	"	1 John		Do	
	385	1	"	"	1 Peter Samsay		Do	
	386	2	"	"	1 John Bright		Do	
	387	2	"	1	" Jim Mammah		Do	
	388	2	"	"	1 William Macauley		Farmer	
	389	2	"	"	1 John George		Do	
	390	"	"	"	1 John Pate		Labour	
	391	1	"	"	1 Peter John		Do	
	392	"	"	"	1 Sam Joe		Do	
	393	1	"	"	1 Joe Dick		Do	
	394	1	"	"	1 Sam Dick		Do	
		541	3	11	377	394	—	

64

	Liberated African Apprentices		Survivors of apprentices living with the inhabitants until their domestic are finished		Natives of the country brought to the colony by the inhabitants of the District		Liberated African children who are too young to be apprenticed and placed at school		Total Population		Stock								Remarks
emales	Males	Females	Males	Females	Males	Females	Males	Females	Males	Females	Horses	Asses	Cows	Oxen	Sheep	Goats	Pigs	Heads of Poultry	
175	74	30	26	14	"	"	"	"	621	574	"	"	16	"	24	15	233	490	
1	1	"	"	"	"	"	"	"	3	2	"	"	"	"	"	"	3	6	
"	1	"	"	"	"	"	"	"	3	1	"	"	"	"	"	"	4	"	
"	"	"	"	"	"	"	"	"	1	1	"	"	"	"	"	"	"	3	
"	"	"	"	"	"	"	"	"	2	1	"	"	"	"	"	"	"	"	
"	"	"	"	"	"	"	"	"	1	1	"	"	"	"	"	"	11	10	
"	"	"	"	"	"	"	"	"	1	1	"	"	"	"	"	"	"	"	
"	"	"	"	"	"	"	"	"	1	"	"	"	"	"	"	"	"	4	
"	"	"	1	"	"	"	"	"	2	1	"	"	"	"	"	"	"	"	
"	"	"	1	"	"	"	"	"	2	1	"	"	"	"	"	"	2	"	
"	"	"	"	"	"	"	"	"	1	1	"	"	"	"	"	"	"	"	
"	"	"	"	"	"	"	"	"	1	"	"	"	"	"	"	"	"	"	
"	"	"	1	"	"	"	"	"	2	"	"	"	"	"	"	"	"	"	
"	"	"	"	"	"	"	"	"	1	"	"	"	"	"	"	"	"	"	
"	2	"	"	1	"	"	"	"	4	2	"	"	"	"	"	1	"	12	
"	1	"	"	"	"	"	"	"	3	1	"	"	"	"	"	"	2	3	
"	"	"	"	"	"	"	"	"	1	"	"	"	"	"	"	"	"	"	
1	1	"	"	"	"	"	"	"	2	2	"	"	"	"	"	"	"	"	
"	"	"	"	"	"	"	"	"	1	"	"	"	"	"	"	"	"	"	
"	"	"	"	"	"	"	"	"	1	1	"	"	"	"	"	"	"	"	
"	"	"	1	"	"	"	"	"	2	1	"	"	"	"	"	"	4	4	
"	"	"	2	"	"	"	"	"	3	1	"	"	"	"	1	"	"	"	
1	1	"	"	"	"	"	"	"	2	2	"	"	"	"	"	"	"	7	
3	0	"	"	"	"	"	"	"	2	4	"	"	"	"	"	"	"	6	
1	0	"	"	"	"	"	"	"	1	2	"	"	"	"	"	"	"	"	
"	"	"	"	"	"	"	"	"	1	1	"	"	"	"	"	"	"	"	
"	"	"	"	"	"	"	"	"	1	"	"	"	"	"	"	"	"	"	
"	"	"	"	"	"	"	"	"	1	1	"	"	"	"	"	"	1	4	
"	"	"	"	"	"	"	"	"	1	1	"	"	"	"	"	"	3	4	
182	81	30	32	15	"	"	"	"	668	548	"	"	16	"	25	16	263	552	

Village or hamlet	Town or Country Allotment No.	Houses			Name of Proprietor		By how many Persons	Trade or General Occupation
			Stone	Frame	Liberated African	Disbd. Soldier		
	541	3	11	377	394	—		
	395	2	"	"	1 Thomas Bates			Labourer
	396	2	"	"	1 Tom Freeman			Do
	397	1	"	"	1 William Johnson			Do
	398	2	"	"	1 Peter Hazeley			Farmer
	399	2	"	"	1 William Foulah			Do
	400	2	"	"	1 Dick Robinson			Do
	401	0	"	"	1 James Sunnay			Shoemaker
Regent—continued	402	2	"	"	1 John Freeman			Sawyer
	403	13	"	1	" Edward Perry			Labourer
	404	2	"	"	1 Osam			Farmer
	405	2	"	"	1 Joe Parkinson			Do
	406	2	"	"	1 William Parkinson			Do
	407	2	"	"	1 John Thomas			Do
	408	2	"	"	1 Richard Cramp			Do
	409	2	"	"	1 Thomas Buck			Sawyer
	410	"	"	"	1 Peter Boocannos			Sawyer
	411	"	"	"	1 George Bull			Carpenter
	412	2	"	"	1 Henry Neakfall			Labourer
	413	1	"	"	1 Thomas Scott			Labourer
	414	2	"	"	1 Thomas Bull			Do
	415	2	"	"	1 George Macauley			Do
	416	2	"	"	1 John Fever			Farmer
	417	2	"	"	1 Annowah			Labourer
	418	0	"	"	" Martin Lathorn			Do
	419	2	"	"	1 Sam Fever			Sawyer
	420	"	"	"	1 Peter Freeman			Labourer
	421	2	"	"	1 Jim Ogoo			Do
	422	1	"	"	1 Jim Parkinson			Farmer
	423	"	"	"	1 Dick Fever			Do
	424	1	"	"	1 John Jackson			Do
	584	3	12	405	424	—		

Okrafo-Smart Family: Over a Century in the Lives of a Liberated African Family

Okrafo-Smart Family: Over a Century in the Lives of a Liberated African Family

Village or Hamlet	Town or Country allotment / No. of acres	House / Stone / Frame / Mud	Name of Proprietor — Liberated African	By how many — Disch'd Soldier	Town or Cens. Occup.
	5843 / 3 / 12 / 405		424	—	
	425 / 2 / " / "		1 Jim Boocanno		Labour
	426 / " / " / "		1 John Gomokoo		Do
	427 / 1 / " / "		1 Aray		Do
	428 / " / " / "		1 Dick Durham		Do
	429 / 1 / " / "		1 Acoree		Do
	430 / 3 / " / "		1 David Nixon		Do
	431 / 2 / " / "		1 Sam John		Do
	432 / 2 / " / "		1 Dick Bull		Do
	433 / 1 / " / "		1 Peter Kendall		Do
	434 / 1 / " / "		1 William Pitt		Do
Regent Hartland	435 / 2 / " / "		1 Tom William		Do
	436 / 1 / " / "		1 Jim Richard		Agricul
	437 / 1 / " / "		1 Oggieboo		Labour
	438 / 2 / " / "		1 James Jay		Sailor
	439 / 2 / " / "		1 Henry Smart		Carpen
	440 / 2 / " / "		1 William Pitt		Labour
	441 / 1 / " / "		1 Eggin		Do
	442 / 2 / " / "		1 Sam Thomas		Farmer
	443 / 2 / " / "		1 Thomas Bates		Do
	444 / 4 / " / "		1 Britain Macauly		Do
	445 / 2 / " / "		1 Ted Macauly		Do
	446 / 2 / " / "		1 Jessy Smart		Do
	447 / 4 / " / 1		1 John Smart		Carpen
	448 / 2 / " / "		1 James Thomas		Farmer
	449 / 2 / " / "		1 John Pitt		Do
	450 / " / " / "		1 Thomas Davis		Do
	451 / 2 / " / "		1 Jessy Collins		Sawy
	452 / 2 / " / "		1 Thomas Bellar		Farmer
	453 / 2 / " / "		1 Abraham John		Do
	454 / 2 / " / "		1 William Peter		Do
	" / 6363 / 3 / 13 / 434		454	"	

```
447
John Smart
Frame House
Carpenter
```

Okrafo-Smart Family: Over a Century in the Lives of a Liberated African Family

Village or Hamlet	Town or Country Residence	Houses	Franked	Grand	Name of Proprietor — Lib.d African	By how many Dec.d Soldier	Trade or General Occupation
	6363	3	13	434	454		
	455	2	"	"	1 Thomas George		Agricult.
	456	2	"	"	1 Peter Nichol		D.o
	457	1	"	"	1 Joseph Appanah		D.o
	458	2	"	"	1 John Fever		D.o
	459	2	"	"	1 Billey George		D.o
	460	2	"	"	1 Ar. Katter		D.o
	461	3	"	"	1 William George		D.o
	462	1	"	"	1 Isaac Davis		D.o
	463	1	"	"	1 Jim Decker		D.o
Regent Continued	464	2	"	"	1 Abraham John 2.d		D.o
	465	2	"	"	1 Geo Bucknor		D.o
	466	3	"	"	1 Sam William		D.o
	467	2	"	"	1 John Weeks		D.o
	468	2	"	"	1 Joe Freeman		D.o
	469	1	"	"	1 John Davis		Mas.
	470	1	"	"	1 John Farmer		Farm.
	471	2	"	1	. Jones Ball		Carpen.
	472	1	"	"	1 Sam Perry		Farmer
	473	2	"	"	1 Jim Shaw		D.o
	474	1	"	"	1 Sam Collins		Mas.
	475	2	"	"	1 Abraham Hughes		Mas.
	476	2	"	"	1 John Poate		Carpen.
	477	1	"	"	1 Jim Maccondo		Farmer
	478	.	"	1	. Thomas Morgan		Carpen.
	479	2	"	"	1 James Fa.		Farmer
	480	3	"	"	1 Thomas B Johnson		Sail.
	481	1	"	"	1 Thomas Johnson		Labour
	482	1	"	"	1 Matthew Deford		Mas.
	483	2	"	"	1 Lewis Way		Sail.
	484	1	"	"	1 John Wickebash		Lab.
	6853	3	15	462	484		

Okrafo-Smart Family: Over a Century in the Lives of a Liberated African Family

Okrafo-Smart Family: Over a Century in the Lives of a Liberated African Family

Village or Hamlet	Town or country &c	Acres	House Stone	House Frame	House Grass	Name of Proprietor — Liberated African / Disch? Soldier	By how many	Trade or Genl Occupa...
		685½	3	15	462	484		
		485	2	"	"	1 Thomas Green		Shingler
		486	2	"	"	1 Abraham Johnson		Mas...
		487	1	"	"	1 Adam Beckett		Shoem...
		488	1	"	"	1 Ogha		Agricult...
		489	2	"	1	" James Bell		Mas...
		490	1	"	"	1 Peter Macauley		Do
		491	2	"	"	1 Abraham Peter		Do
Agent Continued		492	2	"	"	1 John Teffell		Goale...
		493	1	"	"	1 Tom Cock		Agricul...
		494	1	"	"	1 William Neil		Carpen...
		495	1	"	"	1 Thomas Ajah		Carpen...
		496	1	"	"	1 Martha Kingtall		Spin...
		497	2	"	"	1 William Johnson		Sawy...
		498	2	"	"	1 John Peter		Sawy...
		499	13	"	"	1 William Buckhor		Do
		500	2	"	"	1		Carpen...
		501	1	"	"	1 Thomas ...		Farme...
		502	3	"	"	1 Peter Johnson		Do
		503	3	"	"	1 William Greenwood		Do
		504	3	"	"	1 Tom John		Do
		505	2	"	"	1 Congah		Do
		506	2	"	"	1 Arkarrah		Do
		507	1	"	"	1 Achan		Do
		508	1	"	"	1 Affochauray		Do
		509	1	"	"	1 Sam John		Do
		510	1	"	"	1 Sam Peter		Do
		511	"	"	"	1 Adam Coombah		Labou...
			"	"	"	" Samuel Crowther		Schoolm...
			"	"	"	" Edward Bickersteth		Teach...
							4	4
		727	3	16	488	513		

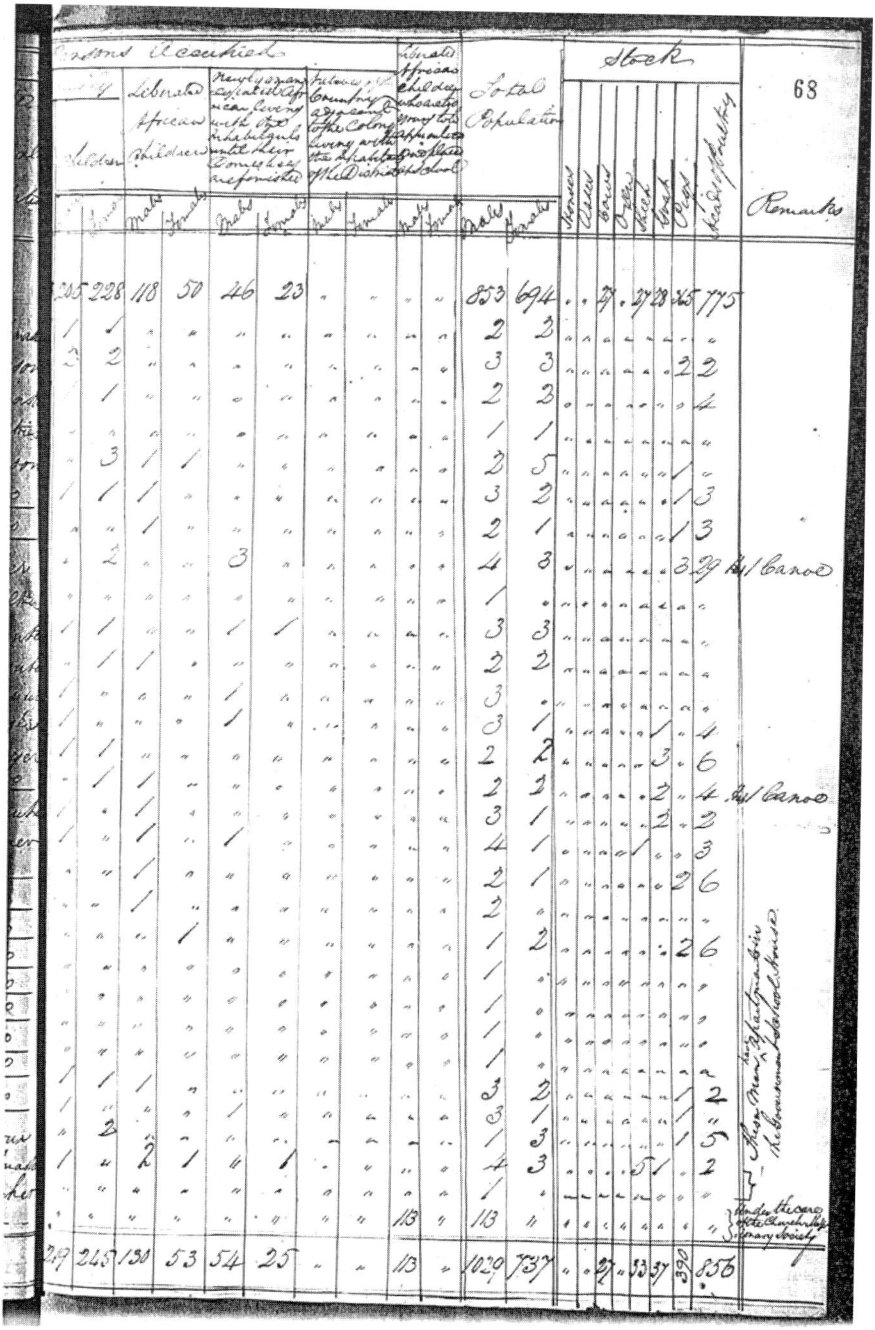

Okrafo-Smart Family:
Over a Century in the Lives of a Liberated African Family

List of Illustrations

Picture Title	Page Number
Cotton Tree Freetown*	Front Cover
Missionaries Travelling in West Africa*	6
Approach to Freetown, Cape Lighthouse*	9
Three Bishops of Freetown	11
Street Preaching – Freetown*	12
Interior of St George's Cathedral, Freetown*	18
Regent Church*	21
Old Fourah Bay College*	37
Daniel Weeks Smart – grandson of Frederick Weeks Smart	93
Mrs. Onike John neé Smart	93
The Old Grammar School, Freetown*	95
Family Ancestors	103
Plate Presented by Mrs. Elizabeth Wellesley-Cole	104
Dr. Benjamin Okrafor-Smart	104
Family Photograph on the occasion of Robert Wellesley-Cole leaving Freetown to study medicine 1928	113
Dr. Robert Wellesley-Cole in gown 1944	114
Dr. Wilfred Jones	115
Doctor (Mrs.) Irene Elizabeth Beatrice Ighodaro (née Wellesley Cole)	122
Francis Weeks Okrafor Smart (my grandfather)	127
The City Hotel	129
OkraforVille – Smart Farm	161
Medal to Commemorate the Centenary Celebrations of Regent Village 1813-1913	171
John Edowu Okrafo-Smart	175
Ejuma Okrafo-Smart	175
Francis Balogun Okrafo-Smart (father)	176
Sarian Okrafo-Smart née England (mother)	176
Oreh William Okrafo-Smart (uncle)	176
Family photograph taken on the 80th birthday of Mrs. Taiwo Sharif née Wellesley-Cole	179

* Pictures supplied by kind permission of Gary Schulze; a wide range of pictures of Sierra Leone can be viewed online at: www.sierra-leone.org

Endnotes

1. Robert Wellesley-Cole; An Innocent In Britain, Campbell Mathers & Co Ltd. London 1988
2. Church Missionary Society Records CA1/0219/61a Journal Extracts for the quarter ending June 1837 by John Weeks
3. Wyse, A; The Krio of Sierra Leone, C Hurst & Company, London, 1989, p2.
4. The Times; 15th April 1830, p3.
5. Church Missionary Society Records CA1/0219/61a Journal Extracts from the Quarter ending June 1837
6. St Petrox Parish Registers Marriages, Births and Deaths 1786 – 1795.
7. Summer, DL; Education in Sierra Leone, The Government of Sierra Leone 1963 p20.
8. Summer, DL; Education in Sierra Leone p14-15
9. Church Missionary Society Records CAI/0219/1 Weeks letter to Bickersteth CMS London. His first letter on arrival in Sierra Leone dated July 10th 1825.
10. Church Missionary Society Records CAI/0219/46 Report of Regent School Quarter ending 25th March 1832 by John Weeks.
11. The Powerful Bond, Hannah Kilham 1774 – 1832 p228
12. The Gentleman's Magazine, London, July 1857 p98, The British Library Document Section Colindale, London.
13. Regent The First Hundred Years, Christopher Fyfe
14. Church Missionary Society Records CA1/0129/106b Journal of voyage to Fernando Po in the months of April, May June 1853
15. Ibid
16. Church Missionary Society Records CA3 036 – Nigeria – Niger Mission 1857-1882
17. Church Missionary Society Records CA3 036
18. Church Missionary Society Records CA3 035 Original Papers – letters and papers of individual missionaries and catechists Reverend Frederick Weeks Smart 1868 – 1880.

19. Church Missionary Society Records CA3/037, No 64 Taylor to Venn 15th December 1866
20. Heslop Library, Birmingham, CAI/023 Letter 77 – Received October 28/76 List III 1870-71 page 323
21. Heslop Library, Birmingham, Ref: CAI/023/84A
22. A History of Sierra Leone, Christopher Fyfe p 425
23. Death of Mr. W S Smart, June 10th 1922, Sierra Leone Weekly News
24. PRO CO267/407 Letter from Acting Governor Crooks to Secretary of State No58 20th February 1894.
25. Letter Sierra Leone No 58 from Administrator W Crooks to the Right Honourable The Marquis of Rippon KG CO267/407 20th February 1894
26. PRO CO 27271 Sierra Leone 1894
27. PRO CO 27271 Sierra Leone 1894
28. An Innocent in Britain; Robert Wellesley-Cole, Campbell Matthew & Co Ltd 1988 p2.
29. West Africa, Current Affairs, Appreciation, 11-17th December 1995
30. West Africa, Current Affairs, Appreciation, 15-2First January 1996
31. The Sierra Leone Weekly News, 6th August 1907
32. The Sierra Leone Weekly News, 3rd November 1906
33. Ibid
34. The Sierra Leone Weekly News, 3rd November 1906
35. The Sierra Leone Weekly News, Freetown, August 14th 1920
36. The Lumbering Trade, The Weekly News March 31, 1906
37. Ibid
38. The Sierra Leone Weekly News, 3First March 1906
39. The Sierra Leone Weekly News, September 1907
40. The Sierra Leone Weekly News, 14th December 1907
41. The Sierra Leone Weekly News, Editorial Comment September 8th 1928
42. The Sierra Leone Weekly News, August 6th 1907.

43. The Sierra Leone Weekly News, 2nd January 1910 F W Okrafor, England's Cattle Farm.
44. The Sierra Leone Weekly News, Editorial Comment on Okrafu's Article February 5th 1910
45. An African Feminist; The Life and Times of Adelaide Smith Ceoly Hayford; 1868-1960 by Adelaide M Cromwell. Harvard University Press, Washington DC 1992 pp12-13
46. Ibid. p15
47. The Sierra Leone Weekly News; August 8th 1907. Our Country – How to Make it Better article by F W Okrafor-Smart.
48. The Sierra Leone Weekly News 1907
49. The Criminal Code, Sierra Leone Weekly News 13th December 1919, F Okrafo-Smart
50. The Sierra Leone Weekly News; Saturday January 25th 1930.
51. The Weekly News September 29th 1923
52. Akintola J G Wyse, H C Bankole-Bright; Politics in Colonial Sierra Leone, 1919-1958, Cambridge University Press, p32.
53. Akintola J G Wyse, H C Bankole-Bright; Politics in Colonial Sierra Leone 1919-1958 Conhugh & Murrough Press 1990 p32
54. Ibid
55. Elementary Education, The Weekly News March 27th 1909
56. The Sierra Leone Weekly News, April 11th 1925
57. The Sierra Leone Weekly News, August 8th 1925
58. Ibid
59. Ibid
60. The Weekly News, Regent Centenary Celebrations November 15th 1913.
61. Regent Centenary Celebrations Programme, Sierra Leone Weekly News November 1913.
62. Centenary Celebrations Making Arrangements, Sierra Leone Weekly News May 25th 1912.

63 Regent Centenary 2nd Anniversary Weekly News November 27th 1915
64 Official Draft Programme of The Visit of H R H The Prince of Wales, The Weekly News January 3rd 1925.
65 Copies from: PRO, CO267/111 Regent Village Census

INDEX

A

Abeokuta · 18
Aboko-Cole
 Mary · 101, 127
Aboli · 33
Abolition · 3, 42
Accra · 28, 89, 90, 91
Adeniyi-Jones · 107
Africa · 7, 10, 2, 4, 7, 21, 24, 36, 68, 87, 101, 104, 107, 111, 115, 117, 119, 121, 122, 123, 124, 140, 144, 155, 157, 167, 168, 221, 224
African bishop · 26
Africanus Horton · 71
Ajayi · 26
Akassa · 61
Akintola Wyse · 1, 158
All Saints Church Yaba · 106
An Innocent in Britain · 7, 115, 121, 224
Anna Pope · 19
Annie Walsh Memorial School · 91, 102, 111, 123
Aunty Oni · 93
Australia · 4, 179
Ayambo · 57

B

Bai Bureh · 148
Banjul · 91, 179
Bathurst Street · 137, 160
Benn · 42
Bishop of Sierra Leone · 12, 15, 17
Bishop Owen Emeric Vidal · 15
Boer War · 104
Bonny · 33, 37, 38, 41, 44, 48, 51, 52, 59, 63, 72, 78, 79, 83, 85, 95
Brass Mission · 44
British Policy of Intervention · 178
Brodie
 Anna Isabel Law · 118
Brother Carew · 46

C

Calabars · 33
Cape Coast Castle · 69
Cape Colony · 4
Cape Mesurado · 22
Cates · 80
Cathedral School · 91
centenary celebrations · 30
Chariff
 Mrs nee Wellesley-Cole · 112
Charles Moore · 44
Charles Shaw · 22
Charlotte Street · 93
Chief Jack William Pepple · 47
Chief Maximillan Pepple · 45
Chief Oke Epella · 56
Christian · 13, 16, 20, 23, 27, 33, 38, 41, 42, 64, 81, 85, 108, 117
Christina Obonne · 73
Christmas Day · 53, 64, 72
Christopher Fyfe · 5, 7, 9, 21, 38, 43, 70, 145, 178, 223, 224, 236
Church Missionary Society · 5, 11, 17, 22, 41, 78, 82, 223, 224, 236
Church of England · 26, 99
City Hotel · 10, 123, 129, 221
Civil war · 48, 129
Clarkson · 3
Clergy Deceased · 17
CMS · 5, 14, 15, 16, 23, 24, 25, 26, 28, 38, 41, 47, 70, 99, 105, 223, 236
Colonel Denham · 2
Colonel Frederic Cardew · 148
Colony · 10, 23, 26, 28, 90, 138, 139, 150, 153, 158, 181
Commodore Cornmerill · 65
Conakry, Guinea · 102
Congo · 27, 38, 108, 164
Constance Cummings-John · 93
Cotton Tree · 1, 19, 221
Criminal Code · 10, 152, 153, 154, 225
Cromwell

Adelaide M · 147

D

Dakar, Guinea · 108
Daniel · 91, 93, 102, 155, 221
Dartmouth · 11
David Livingstone · 42
Dawoda Lane, Ebute Meta · 106
Day
    Alexander · 28
descendants · 13, 29, 157, 179
Devonshire · 31
diabetes · 96
Dr. J Abayomi-Cole · 172
Dr. J K Randle · 158
Dr. Randle · 171
Dr. Robert Wellesley-Cole · 7, 96, 178, 221
During · 61, 142

E

Earl Bathurst · 2
East Street · 92
Ebenezar Lancelot Auber · 160
Ebute Meta Lagos · 106
Edward Beckles · 44
Elizabeth · 10, 122, 221
Ellaline Smart · 93
ENGLANDS CATTLE FARM · 140

F

F W Okrafor Smart · 172
F. Harrison Rankin · 29
F. W. OKRAFO SMART · 169
Fante · 175
Farming · 25
Fernando-Po · 33
Fine Waters at St George's Valley · 159
Fourah Bay College · 37, 105, 108, 117, 119, 123, 124, 221

Fowler
    James · 173
    Francis · 8, 9, 10, 11, 95, 96, 97, 98, 99, 101, 107, 123, 137, 145, 166, 172, 177, 221
    Frederick · 9, 38, 39, 42, 63, 70, 101, 221, 223, 236
Freetown · 5, 7, 10, 1, 2, 4, 9, 12, 13, 18, 22, 25, 28, 31, 32, 37, 77, 82, 89, 90, 91, 92, 93, 99, 102, 106, 108, 116, 117, 119, 122, 123, 124, 129, 130, 135, 145, 148, 149, 150, 153, 155, 157, 159, 160, 163, 167, 174, 175, 176, 177, 178, 221, 224

G

Gambia · 28, 91, 92, 93, 98, 119
George Brook · 159
George III · 22
George, Prince of Wales · 22
Ghana · 9, 4, 90, 175
Gloucester · 28
Goderich Street · 25
Governor Hennessy · 148
Governor T. P. Thompson · 21
Graham Greene's *The Heart of the Matter* · 123
Grammar School · 91, 101, 102, 104, 105, 108, 117, 128, 137, 221
Granville Sharp · 3, 60
Guinea · 4
Gulf of Guinea · 33

H

Hannah Campbell · 30
headman · 7, 28, 31, 33, 35
HIGH SCHOOL · 9, 89
His Majesty the King · 66
Hogbrook · 21, 22
Holy Orders · 16
Holy Trinity church · 25
Honourable M. T. Dawe · 168
hospital · 24, 119, 125, 126
Hut Tax · 148

I

Ibo · 3, 5, 19, 32, 37, 41, 59
Igbo · 24, 27
Ighodaro
   Anthony · 126
   Ayodele · 126
   Oluyinka · 126
   Sam · 112
   Samuel Osarogie · 124
   Wilfred · 126
Imo · 3, 106
Isle-de-Los · 9, 4
Isles de Los · 28, 96, 97
Itu-Isu near Alo-Chukuru · 106
Ivor Smart · 93
Iwammah · 49, 50

J

J During · 62
J W Cole · 130
J White · 62
Jack Brown · 60
Jacob Cole · 32
Jacob W Lewis · 97
Jamaica · 22
John · 3, 7, 8, 9, 11, 13, 17, 34, 95, 98, 155, 177, 182, 221, 223, 236
   Thomas · 28
John Macaulay Wilson · 24
John Smart · 177
John Smart Second · 31, 33
John Weeks · 3, 7, 8, 9, 3, 7, 11, 13, 14, 15, 16, 19, 20, 26, 31, 178, 223, 236
Johnson · 23, 24, 25, 61, 62, 90, 124, 155
   Emma · 108
   Lucy · 173
Jones
   Bishop Percy · 115
   Fiona · 115
   John · 115
   Mai · 115
   Percy · 111
   Sally · 115
   Veronica · 115
Juju · 42, 49, 56, 57, 60, 65
Justina Smart · 90

K

Kahinde · 107
   Ajoke · 107
   Sarah · 107
King George Pepple · 69, 70
King of Kafu Bullom · 24
Kingston-on-Hull · 21
Kossoh Town Boy · 115, 121
Krio · 5, 1, 95, 115, 121, 158, 176, 223, 236
Krios · 14, 138, 153
Kumasi · 71

L

Lagos · 29, 52, 70, 105, 106, 107, 140, 158, 166
Law
   Andrew Bonar · 118
Leicester Mountain · 21
Liberated Africans · 1, 4, 13, 14, 157, 159
Limba · 101, 105, 138
London · 7, 15, 22, 23, 24, 25, 26, 33, 37, 38, 41, 70, 77, 78, 87, 114, 115, 117, 118, 119, 121, 124, 149, 178, 223, 236
   Pentonville · 4

M

Macauley · 3, 42, 171
   Samuel · 173
MacCarthy · 22, 24, 27, 29
magistrate · 23, 98
Major W. J. Ross · 30
Manufacturing Company Ltd · 130
Maria Louisa Charlesworth · 24
Maroon settlers · 22
marriage · 19, 80, 93

Mary · 102
Mayoress of Freetown · 93
McGregor Laird Steamship · 52
Methodist · 23, 27
missionaries · 11, 13, 14, 15, 16, 22, 26, 34, 35, 38, 39, 40, 41, 78, 83, 99, 111, 117, 178, 223, 236
Mr. Carew · 62
Mr. Comber · 39, 44
Mr. Consul Livingstone · 65
Mr. J S Labor · 136
Mr. M H Thompson · 173
Mr. Marke · 96
Mr. O J Benjamin · 92
Mr. P Lemberg Mayor · 130
Mr. Thomas · 29
Mr. Uriah Taylor · 102, 108
Mrs. Samuels · 49
Mrs. Weeks · 15

N

Nancy · 25
National Congress of British West Africa · 10, 107, 155, 157
native catechists · 18
native ministry · 18
New Calabar · 65
Newcastle · 105, 114, 118, 119, 123
Nicol
    Pompey · 27
Niger Expedition · 18
Niger Mission · 9, 28, 32, 33, 34, 35, 37, 40, 41, 62, 77, 78, 82, 84, 87, 89, 90, 91, 223, 236
Nigeria · 5, 7, 1, 3, 4, 5, 9, 18, 19, 24, 33, 34, 35, 37, 38, 40, 77, 78, 101, 105, 106, 115, 119, 120, 122, 124, 125, 166, 179, 223, 236
NOTES ON AGRICULTURE · 162
Nottingham General Hospital · 115

O

Oko Jumbo · 65
Okorafor

Francis · 4
Okorafo-Smart
    Francis · 108, 109, 111, 127, 129, 130, 133, 137, 139, 149, 150, 153, 154, 155, 157, 158, 159, 160, 161
Okoroafor · 7, 9, 3, 4, 5, 7, 13, 106, 177
Okoroafor-Smart · 4, 7
Okrafo · 5
Okrafor-Smart · 8, 3, 5, 105, 127
    Ayomi · 175, 176
    Benjamin · 104
    Daniel · 107
    Francis · 154, 157, 158
    Francis Balogun · 175
    Frederick · 102
    Jaydee · 175
    John · 104
    John Edowu · 175
    Leonora · 175
    Melissa · 175
    Olivia · 175
    Oreh William · 175
OkraforVille · 160
Okrafo-Smart
    Benjamin · 176
    Elizabeth Beatrice · 111
    Florence · 176
    Frances · 176
    Francis · 172, 173, 175, 176
    Rachel Adjuah · 175
    Sylvia · 176
    Victor · 2, 5, 70, 176
    Winston · 176
Okrika · 65
Onike · 91, 93, 221
Onitsha · 28, 33, 35, 92
Orlu Division in Imo · 106

P

P Lemberg · 130
Pademba Road · 28, 89
Peter Hughes · 25, 26
Phoebe · 115
Phoebe Graham · 15, 19
Pilot Johnson · 90

Okrafo-Smart Family: Over a Century in the Lives of a Liberated African Family

polygamy · 2, 41
Poso · 57
Pratt
    Ejuma · 175
PRIMER · 37
Prince Regent · 22
Princes Henry and Charles · 69
Professor S Ferrier · 145

R

Randle · 92
    Dr John · 29
Regent · 3, 7, 9, 10, 11, 3, 5, 6, 12, 13, 15, 16, 19, 21, 22, 23, 24, 25, 26, 27, 28, 29, 30, 31, 32, 33, 35, 38, 78, 87, 91, 92, 99, 102, 104, 106, 108, 111, 128, 134, 172, 173, 178, 181, 182, 221, 223, 225, 226, 236
Regent Centenary Celebrations · 10, 171, 173, 221, 225
Regina Williams · 91
Reginald Smart · 93
Rev. A E Williams · 172
Rev. T S Johnson · 172
Reverend D C Crowther · 53
Reverend D L Crowther · 63
Reverend Dandeson Crowther · 39
Reverend E Jones · 32
Reverend E N Jones · 7
Reverend Edmonson · 128
Reverend Edward Bickersteth · 23
Reverend Frederick Smart · 77, 90
Reverend Frederick Weeks Smart · 28
Reverend George Crowley Nicol · 27
Reverend H J Alcock · 77, 79
Reverend J Johnson · 63
Reverend James White · 63
Reverend John Bowen · 18
Reverend John Weeks · 13
Reverend John William Weeks · 17, 18
Reverend Joseph During · 63
Reverend N H Boston · 171
Reverend Nathaniel Denton · 27
Reverend R P Crabbe · 172
Reverend Simeon Smart · 28
Reverend T.E. Poole · 29

Reverend W Morgan · 63
Reverend Wright · 78
Reverends W Morgan · 62
Right Honourable The Marquis of Ripon KG · 96
River Niger · 52

S

S S *'Congo'* · 51
Samuel Crowther · 26
Samuel Smart · 3, 4
Sarian England · 176
Sawyer
    Temne · 28
Sherbro Mendi · 138
Sierra Leone · 3, 5, 7, 8, 10, 1, 3, 7, 9, 11, 12, 14, 15, 17, 18, 19, 22, 26, 28, 29, 35, 38, 44, 51, 53, 77, 82, 83, 85, 87, 91, 92, 93, 97, 99, 104, 105, 106, 107, 108, 111, 114, 115, 117, 119, 120, 121, 122, 128, 130, 134, 135, 136, 137, 138, 139, 140, 144, 145, 146, 147, 149, 150, 151, 152, 153, 155, 157, 158, 160, 161, 163, 166, 167, 168, 173, 174, 176, 177, 178, 179, 222, 223, 224, 225, 236
Sierra Leone Industrial and Development Company · 136
Sierra LeoneWeekly News · 90, 91, 92, 105, 106, 107, 128, 130, 132, 135, 137, 138, 139, 145, 146, 147, 150, 151, 153, 158, 161, 166, 167, 168, 169, 174, 224, 225, 226
Sir Charles MacCarthy · 22
Sir F Fleming · 96
Sir Garnet Wolseley · 70
Sir Thomas Fowell Buxton · 60
slave ships · 1, 21, 24
slave trade · 1, 12
Smart · 2, 5, 7, 9, 10, 11, 4, 5, 13, 18, 19, 28, 32, 33, 34, 35, 37, 53, 70, 81, 82, 86, 87, 88, 89, 90, 92, 93, 95, 96, 97, 98, 104, 105, 106, 107, 123, 137, 162, 167, 169, 172, 177, 182, 221, 223, 224, 225, 236
    Anthony · 108

Christian Jackson Adjou · 108
Daniel Augustus · 108
Frederick · 41, 77, 78, 108
Frederick and Francis · 35
John · 5, 177
Mary · 173
Mrs · 56, 60
Smart Farm · 159, 160, 161, 170
Somerset · 3
South Africa · 7
SS · 61
St Charles · 12, 22, 104
St Charles' Church · 173
St George's Cathedral · 18, 221
St Petrox, Devon · 20
St Stephen's Church · 37
Stanley the famous explorer · 70
Susan Crowther · 28
Susu · 138
Sylvanus Smart · 92

T

T J Thompson; *The Jubilee and Centenary Volume of Fourah Bay College* · 108
Temne · 30, 138
The Ashanti Expedition · 69, 70
The Weekly News · 90, 128, 130, 224, 225, 226
The White Mans Grave · 15
Thomas · 42, 155
Thomas Hirst · 23
Thomas Peter J C · 123
Toro-dig-bo · 66
Transportation Company of Freetown · 135
twins · 7, 19, 35, 175, 177, 178

U

University of Durham · 105, 123

V

Vai · 22
Vicar of St Thomas, Lambeth · 15
Vice-Admiralty Court · 22
villages · 22, 23, 26, 29, 30, 33, 53, 172, 181, 182

W

W N Thomas · 130
W P Golley · 130
W T Prout · 130
Waterloo · 32
Weeks · 2, 7, 8, 9, 4, 5, 7, 11, 13, 14, 16, 17, 18, 19, 26, 27, 37, 105, 178, 182, 221, 223, 236
  Elizabeth · 20
  John · 5, 14, 20
  William · 20
Weeks Okrafor-Smart
  Francis · 127, 160
Weeks Smart
  Alfred Benjamin · 108
  Francis · 19
  Frederick · 19, 47
Wellesley-Cole
  Amy Hotobah-During · 115
  Arthur Bandford Ageh · 111
  Elizabeth · 104
  Elizabeth Beatrice · 111
  Eric Soloman Ageh · 112
  Irene Beatrice · 112
  Josephine · 116
  Mabel Taiwo · 112
  Ohodae · 116
  Olivia · 116
  Patrice · 115
  Phoebe Winifred Elizabeth · 111
  Richard · 115, 160
  Robert · 7, 96, 111, 114, 115, 117, 122, 123, 149, 160, 178, 221, 223, 224, 236
  Robert Benjamin Ageh · 111
  Shola · 115
  Tunde · 116

Wilfred · 102, 111, 115, 116, 122, 130, 136, 155, 172, 221
Wilfred Ageh · 111
Wilfred Sydney · 111
Ziporah · 116
Werepe · 166
William · 11, 17, 92, 221
William Augustine Johnson · 23
William Banjo · 45
William Wilberforce · 3, 60
Winwood Reade · 29

Y

Yalinka · 105
Yoruba · 26, 27, 28, 77
Yoruba Mission · 17

Z

Zein Smart · 93
Zulu Wars · 148